Second Edition

W9-ATN-013

Guiding Readers Through Text

Strategy Guides for New Times

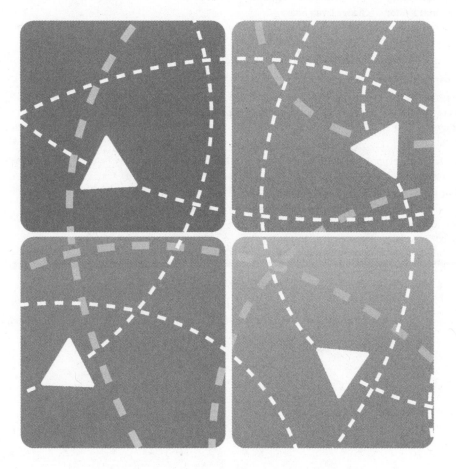

Karen D. Wood ▸ Diane Lapp
James Flood ▸ D. Bruce Taylor

International Reading Association
800 BARKSDALE ROAD, PO BOX 8139
NEWARK, DE 19714-8139, USA
www.reading.org

The International Reading Association attempts, through its publications, to provide a forum for a wide spectrum of opinions on reading. This policy permits divergent viewpoints without implying the endorsement of the Association.

Executive Editor, Books   Corinne M. Mooney
Developmental Editor   Charlene M. Nichols
Developmental Editor   Tori Mello Bachman
Developmental Editor   Stacey Lynn Sharp
Editorial Production Manager   Shannon T. Fortner
Design and Composition Manager   Anette Schuetz

Project Editors   Stacey Lynn Sharp and Cynthia L. Held

Cover Design   Lise Holliker Dykes

Library of Congress Cataloging-in-Publication Data

Guiding readers through text : strategy guides for new times / Karen D. Wood ... [et al.]. -- 2nd ed.
    p. cm.
  First ed. entered under: Wood, Karen D.
  Includes bibliographical references and index.
  ISBN 978-0-87207-681-5
  1. Reading--Aids and devices. 2. Reading comprehension. I. Wood, Karen D.
  LB1573.39.W66 2007
  428.4071--dc22

                                                                                    2007040934

CONTENTS ▶▶▷

Karen D. Wood received her PhD from the University of Georgia in Athens, Georgia, USA, and is currently a professor in the Department of Reading and Elementary Education at the University of North Carolina at Charlotte, North Carolina, USA. A former middle school reading teacher and K–12 literacy specialist in the public schools, she is the author of more than 175 articles, chapters, and books focusing on various topics including integrating literacy across the curriculum, meeting the needs of diverse learners, vocabulary and comprehension development, and translating research and theory into classroom practice. These articles have appeared in journals such as *The Reading Teacher, Journal of Reading, Reading and Writing Quarterly, Reading Psychology, Language Arts*, and the *Middle School Journal*. Wood originated the Research Into Practice column for the *Middle School Journal* in 1986 and continues as its author today.

She was a member of the authorship team of the McGraw-Hill basal reading series from 1989–2004 and was the former coeditor of *Reading Research and Instruction*. Her most recent books include *Integrating Reading and Writing in Middle and Secondary Classrooms, Teaching Literacy in the Sixth Grade, Promoting Literacy in Grades 4–9: A Handbook for Teachers and Administrators, Literacy Strategies Across the Subject Areas* (2nd ed.), *Instructional Strategies for Teaching Content Vocabulary*, and *Promoting Literacy With Adolescent Learners: Research-Based Instruction* (in press).

Diane Lapp, EdD, is Distinguished Professor of Education in the Department of Teacher Education at San Diego State University (SDSU), California, USA, and has taught in elementary and middle schools. In addition to her university work, she is currently teaching a special section of English at San Diego High School in San Diego, California. Her major areas of research and instruction have been on issues related to struggling readers who live in urban settings and their families. Lapp directs and teaches field-based preservice and graduate programs and courses and continues to team-teach in public school classrooms. She has authored, coauthored, and edited numerous articles, columns, texts, handbooks, and children's materials on reading and language arts issues, including the following: *Teaching Reading to Every Child*, a reading methods textbook in its fourth edition; *Content Reading & Learning* (3rd ed.); *Accommodating Language Differences Among English Language Learners: 75 Strategy Lessons* (2nd ed.); *The Handbook of Research in Teaching the English Language Arts* (2nd ed.); and *The Handbook of Research on Teaching Literacy Through the Communicative and Visual Arts* (2nd ed.).

Lapp has chaired and cochaired several International Reading Association (IRA) and National Reading Conference (NRC) committees and is currently the chair of IRA's Early Literacy Committee. Her many educational awards include being named Outstanding Teacher Educator and Faculty Member in the Department of Teacher Education at SDSU, named the Distinguished Research Lecturer from SDSU's Graduate Division of Research, and named IRA's 1996 Outstanding Teacher Educator of the Year as well as being selected as a member of the California and the International Reading Association halls of fame. Lapp served as the coeditor of California's literacy journal *The California Reader* from 2001–2007.

James Flood, PhD, was Distinguished Professor of Education at San Diego State University (SDSU), California, USA; taught in preschool, elementary, and secondary schools; and was a language arts supervisor and vice principal. He was also a Fulbright scholar at the University of Lisbon in Portugal and the President of the National Reading Conference in the United States. Flood chaired and cochaired many International Reading Association (IRA), National Council of Teachers of English (NCTE), National Council of Research in Education (NCRE), and National Reading Council (NRC) committees. Most recently, Flood taught graduate courses at SDSU.

Flood coauthored and edited many articles, columns, texts, handbooks, and children's materials on reading and language arts issues, including the following (which were codeveloped with Diane Lapp): *Content Area Reading and Learning*, which is in its second edition, and *The Handbook of Research on Teaching Literacy Through the Communicative and Visual Arts*. His many educational awards include being named Outstanding Teacher Educator in the Department of Teacher Education at SDSU and named the Distinguished Research Lecturer from SDSU's Graduate Division of Research, and Flood was selected as a member of both the California and the International Reading Association halls of fame. He was most recently a coeditor of *The California Reader* and was a past member of the Board of Directors of the International Reading Association.

Bruce Taylor, PhD, is an assistant professor in the Department of Reading and Elementary Education at the University of North Carolina at Charlotte, North Carolina, USA. His research and teaching focus on the social and cultural aspects of literacy and learning of adolescents and, in particular, ways to meet the academic learning needs of diverse and often marginalized students. His work explores the role of diverse texts in content area classrooms and the role of discourse in the lives of adolescents. Recently, he has begun to explore the roles of inquiry and service learning as ways to advance literacy and promote agency among marginalized adolescents. Taylor has had articles published in the *Middle School Journal* and *SIGNAL Journal*, and some upcoming articles will appear in *Reading Psychology* and *Reading and Writing Quarterly*. He has coauthored several book chapters and with Karen Wood has coauthored *Literacy Strategies Across the Subject Areas* (2nd ed.).

Taylor teaches graduate and undergraduate courses that focus on content area literacy, multiliteracies, and sociocultural perspectives of language and literacy. A graduate of the University of Iowa in Iowa City, Iowa, USA, Taylor was an English language arts teacher in both urban and rural schools in Texas.

Author Information for Correspondence and Workshops

Karen D. Wood can be contacted at kdwood@uncc.edu.
Diane Lapp can be contacted at lapp@mail.sdsu.edu.
Bruce Taylor can be contacted at dbtaylor@uncc.edu.

Reading the text of *Guiding Readers Through Text: Strategy Guides for New Times* opened up a floodgate of memories for me, both professional and personal. It immediately brought me back to 1970, the year I began my doctoral studies in reading education at Syracuse University in Syracuse, New York, USA. It was a glorious time in my life. My mentor, Hal Herber, had just published his seminal textbook, *Teaching Reading in the Content Areas*. Hal had taken the notion of "reading guides" to a new conceptual and theoretical level. The concept of reading guidance had been around for several decades, but often a "study guide" meant giving students a set of questions to answer after they had read a text selection. Study guides were well-intentioned but often fell short of modeling *how* students needed to read informational text to fully comprehend potentially difficult material in various content areas.

Herber, however, felt that a reading guide should—as its name suggests—*guide* a reader through the processes required to comprehend text effectively. A well-constructed reading guide not only helps students acquire information but also walks them through the thoughtful, strategic processes by which they acquire information and develop concepts at various levels of comprehension. While at Syracuse University in the early 1970s, I was part of a rich tradition of doctoral students who were assigned to the Reading Research Center to develop and research the effectiveness of various types of process-centered reading guides. Needless to say, I built a career in the field of literacy education on my early experiences with reading guides and Herber's theoretical constructs of reading guidance in content areas.

Yet times change. The world of content area teaching and learning that I was introduced to in the 1970s had at its core single-text learning. Reading and study guides were often designed by teachers for separate assignments in 600- to 1,000-page textbooks designed for content area instruction. The textbook still plays an important role in the lives of today's students, but it's not the only show in town anymore. As the authors of *Guiding Readers Through Text* so adroitly explain, technological advances brought on by the digital forces of the computer have transformed the way we communicate and construct knowledge. We live and learn in "new times."

Just as Hal Herber brought reading guides to a new level in the 1970s, I believe that my colleagues Karen Wood, Diane Lapp, Jim Flood, and Bruce Taylor have retooled the study guide concept to a new level of application for new times. Under their thoughtful scholarship, the study guide has morphed into the *strategy guide* to meet the cognitive and strategic demands inherent in a variety of electronic texts constructed and displayed on computer screens and other multimedia. The authors have performed an extraordinary service to the education community. Preservice and inservice teachers will find this book one of the best and most practical instructional resources for content area literacy and learning in the field today.

The memories keep coming as I pore through the pages of this book. Probably the most heartfelt is that of my friend, Jim Flood, whose legacy in the field of literacy will outlive us all. Jim was the real deal—a teacher's teacher, a scholar's scholar, a friend's friend. His smile is felt everywhere in this book. Thanks, Jim, for touching my life on your way to something bigger and better.

—Richard T. Vacca
Past President, International Reading Association
Professor Emeritus, Kent State University

It has been more than 15 years since the first edition of *Guiding Readers Through Text* (Wood, Lapp, & Flood, 1992) was published by the International Reading Association. When we first decided to write this book, the field of reading was experiencing an influx of books and publications on the importance of integrating literacy across the content areas. That interest has not waned but has continued throughout the professional literature today. What has changed, however, is the way in which content area knowledge is disseminated. In the 1990s, the primary purveyor of knowledge was the textbook, the basal reader, or the literature anthology. While those information sources still exist and are certainly in use today, no longer are our classrooms single-textbook classrooms. The field of education, mirroring the world in general, is in a rapid state of technological change. Now our students have many places to go to answer their questions and explore topics in more detail: from Web logs (blogs) to websites to instant messaging and virtual worlds, to name a few.

With the vast array of communication technologies available to students, we saw the need to change the focus of this text. Instead of single-textbook study guides, we see these guides as an opportunity to take students outside of a chapter and into multiple sources of information: touring a virtual world, communicating via e-mail, or gaining a deeper understanding of a concept through an online encyclopedia. When study guides were first advocated in the professional literature on reading, they were essentially a series of questions students had to answer while they were reading a textbook chapter. As the name implied, they helped students "study" what they needed to know for a subsequent test. They were also applied almost exclusively to high school–level material. Similar to the first edition of *Guiding Readers Through Text*, we see guides as appropriate tools for all grade levels. Unlike the first edition, however, the guides in the second edition help teachers and students capitalize on the wide range of information sources now available to them, focusing on the current multiliteracies approach to learning.

To that end, we borrowed Luke and Elkins's (1998) term "New Times" to illustrate the changing face of guides in the classroom. We also see these guides as vehicles to "bridge" print literacies to digital literacies, providing a multimodal transformation for engaging all levels of learners—most of whom use the Internet daily as a way of life (O'Brien, 2007). With the increasing emphasis on the need to develop strategic readers and writers, we have also changed the name "study guide" to "strategy guide" and illustrate how our Phased Transfer Model with flexible grouping (Wood, 2002) can be used as a means of scaffolding new learning under the influence of sociocultural theory and research (Blanton, Wood, & Taylor, 2007; Vygotsky, 1934/1978).

We have also updated these guides to help students develop what we know from the current research (e.g., Gambrell, Morrow, & Pressley, 2007; Pressley, 2000, 2006) to be effective strategies for comprehending: summarizing, visualizing, retelling, creating analogies, reading between the lines, processing and analyzing the content, and engaging in what Allington (2006) terms "thoughtful literacy." By adhering to the Phased Transfer Model with flexible grouping mentioned previously, teachers can begin by demonstrating, explaining, and thinking aloud the strategies elicited through the guides' questions, activities, and statements. Then, teachers can assign students to work in pairs or groups to construct and discuss answers, in essence participating in a "cognitive apprenticeship" phase (Pearson & Fielding, 1991), and finally release them to use and apply these strategies on their own. The end goal of all instruction, as Pearson's work (Pearson & Fielding, 1991; Pearson & Gallagher, 1983) has suggested, is to make the teacher obsolete and to make the student a strategic reader.

Our purpose in this book is to present a comprehensive review of available guides but to recast them as a means of developing strategic readers and writers. We include traditional "study guides" such as the Collaborative Listening–Viewing Guide and Pattern Guide, which have been used by teachers and students for many years. However, we also introduce new guides such as the Inquiry Guide (I-Guide) as a means of answering questions using varied sources of information; the Critical Profiler Guide, designed to help students take a critical stance while reading; and the Foldable Guide, a type of manipulative guide to provide a tactile and visual support for reading and learning. We've provided descriptions and examples of each to help teachers decide which ones to use and when to use them.

Who Should Read This Book

This book is for teachers at all grade levels and all subject areas and, to that end, we have provided an array of examples spanning possible topics across the curriculum. Preservice teachers, practicing teachers, literacy specialists, curriculum coordinators, and administrators will likely find something in this book that meets a need for students they know and want to assist. While guides were originally envisioned as aids for struggling readers, most of the guides in the book can be used with students who have a range of proficiencies. In addition, most of the guides can be adapted for subjects from history to mathematics to literature and English language arts to social studies and science. They can also be used with art classes, health, music, and the vocational fields.

How to Use This Book

This book is designed as a resource, a kind of handbook, for making instructional decisions about the best approaches to use in given lessons. Although teachers may elect to do so, the book is not specifically designed to be read cover to cover. We envisioned that teachers would examine their instructional objectives, analyze the needs of their students, determine the content and resources needed, and then select the guide or guides that will help students achieve their potential. To that end, we begin each chapter with the grade levels for which we think the guide is most suited, the appropriate subject areas, and the classroom context. This last area refers to the method of presentation: whole class, small group, pairs, or individuals. We advocate and recommend that strategy guides not be completed in isolation. They are vehicles for learning, remembering, and reflecting upon new content and work best when students are allowed to interact and discuss the information with one another.

Each chapter describes a specific guide, its history (if appropriate), and research base or rationale, and then proceeds to a description of how to use the guide in a classroom setting. We have included at least one sample lesson for each guide and, in most cases, examples of student responses. Then, at the end of the description, we include a section of Tips for Diverse Learners—a few tried-and-true suggestions for helping not only English-language learners, but also learners representing all dimensions of diversity.

All of these guides have been tried out in classrooms, many by teachers ranging all grade levels and subject areas, so we are confident about their effectiveness as instructional tools. We encourage teachers to adapt the guides, to make changes as they deem necessary to meet the needs of their particular students and lesson. We recommend that all users of this book read the General Guidelines for Classroom Use section beginning on page 24 in chapter 2. Here we provide some generic suggestions for the use of strategy guides, encompassing concerns teachers may have about issues such as grading and grouping students, designing creative guides, and using the guides as a means to attain the end goal of developing strategic readers. The Appendix of the book contains some reproducible masters that we feel can be used as shown or adapted for multiple purposes and texts.

Acknowledgments

We want to give special thanks to a number of teachers and students who have helped with this project. First on our list are doctoral student Charlotte Mecklenburg and high school teacher—and now colleague— Jean Vintinner. Another special thank you needs to go to University of

North Carolina at Charlotte (UNCC) graduate student and high school social studies teacher Aimee Alder. The following are other students and teachers who have made contributions to this work: Lina Soares and Joyce Brigman, doctoral students in Curriculum and Instruction and academic facilitators with Charlotte Mecklenburg Schools; Sara Smith, a high school teacher and graduate student at UNCC; Cindy Hovis and Robin Albrecht, master's degree students and teachers in Lincoln County, North Carolina; Jeanette Burghardt, UNCC graduate student and teacher in Charlotte; Katie Hunter, teacher in Cabarrus County Schools, North Carolina; UNCC preservice teachers Alicia Jones, Jessica Bridges, Shannon Burpeau, and Schuyler Quinley; Rosalind Crandell, UNCC supervisor of teachers; Susan Avett, of Cabarrus County Schools; and Katie Keller Dugan, teacher in the Virginia Public Schools. We also want to thank Valerie Molbert, English preservice teacher and student of Dr. Janis Harmon at the University of Texas at San Antonio, and Rebecca Calloway, teacher in San Diego, California, for their contributions.

REFERENCES

Allington, R. (2006). *What really matters for struggling readers: Designing research-based programs* (2nd ed.). Boston: Allyn & Bacon.

Blanton, W.E., Wood, K.D., & Taylor, D.B. (2007). Rethinking middle school reading instruction: A basic literacy activity. *Reading Psychology, 28,* 75–95.

Gambrell, L.B., Morrow, L.M., & Pressley, M. (2007). *Best practices in literacy instruction* (3rd ed.). New York: Guilford.

Luke, A., & Elkins, J. (1998). Reinventing literacy in "New Times." *Journal of Adolescent & Adult Literacy, 42,* 4–7.

O'Brien, D. (2007, May). *Bridging print literacies and digital literacies in engaging struggling adolescents.* Paper presented at the 52nd annual convention of the International Reading Association, Toronto, ON.

Pearson, P.D., & Fielding, L. (1991). Comprehension instruction. In R. Barr, M.L. Kamil, P. Mosenthal & P.D. Pearson (Eds.), *Handbook of reading research* (Vol. II, pp. 819–860). New York: Longman.

Pearson, P.D., & Gallagher, M.C. (1983). The instruction of reading comprehension. *Contemporary Educational Psychology, 8,* 317–344.

Pressley, M. (2000). What should comprehension instruction be the instruction of? In M.L. Kamil, P.B. Mosenthal, P.D. Pearson & R. Barr (Eds.), *Handbook of reading research* (Vol. III, pp. 545–561). Mahwah, NJ: Erlbaum.

Pressley, M. (2006). *Reading instruction that works: The case for balanced teaching* (3rd ed.). New York: Guilford.

Vygotsky, L.S. (1978). *Mind in society: The development of higher psychological processes* (M. Cole, V. John-Steiner, S. Scribner, & E. Souberman, Eds. & Trans.). Cambridge, MA: Harvard University Press. (Original work published 1934)

Wood, K.D. (2002). Differentiating reading and writing lessons to promote content learning. In C.C. Block, L.B. Gambrell, & M. Pressley (Eds.), *Improving comprehension instruction: Rethinking research, theory, and classroom practice* (pp. 155–180). San Francisco: Jossey-Bass; Newark, DE: International Reading Association.

Wood, K.D., Lapp, D., & Flood, J. (1992). *Guiding readers through text: A review of study guides.* Newark, DE: International Reading Association.

PART I

Using Strategy Guides in K–12 Classrooms

In this section, you will learn about the instructional benefits of strategy guides and how to go about selecting and using them in your classroom. Chapter 1 provides an introduction to the concept of strategy guides and discusses the need for traditional study guides to be recast in the light of current influences on education, such as the multiliteracies approach to text and the rise in informational text. You will also learn how strategy guides can be used as vehicles for socially constructed knowledge, and you will discover the role strategy guides can play in the development of strategic readers. In chapter 2, you will learn how to select the right strategy guides for your classroom by analyzing the materials and student needs and finding a guide that will match those materials and student needs. The chapter also illustrates how to model the use of strategy guides with your students and provides specific classroom guidelines for their use.

CHAPTER 1

Introduction: From Study Guides of the Past to Strategy Guides for the Present and Future

Widespread support for the use of the study guide has appeared in almost every book written on content area reading instruction (Alvermann & Phelps, 2001; Lapp, Flood, & Farnan, 2007; Manzo, Manzo, & Thomas, 2004; Vacca & Vacca, 2008). While there is still broad appeal for the use of study guides, the textual landscape in our society and in our schools has undergone radical change. This is evident in the emergence of digital technologies and access of online hypertext. The scholarship on multiliteracies foregrounds the rapid emergence of texts (Cope & Kalantzis, 2000; New London Group, 1996), while more recently, pedagogy has attempted to catch up with the theoretical understanding of this textual revolution (Anstey & Bull, 2006; Karchmer, Mallette, Kara-Soteriou, & Leu, 2005). As we approached the second edition of this book, we tried to take into account the changes in literacy that have occurred over the last decade. First we explain what study guides are and provide evidence supporting the use of study guides. Then we examine the study guide and its role in "new times" (Luke & Elkins, 1998), recasting this instructional tool in the light of current influences on education, such as the multiliteracies approach to text and the rise in informational text. Next we propose that the name "study guide" be changed to "strategy guide" to reflect the major objective of its use, which is to support students as they become strategic readers.

What Are Study Guides?

Study guides—also known as reading guides—are teacher-developed graphic and questioning guides used to help students organize information as a means to comprehend what they are reading. As students respond to the questions or engage in the organizational activities, they are able to arrange information into categories in a visual and succinct manner that supports their learning and studying.

The use of study guides differs in two important respects from the typical practice of asking students to answer the textbook questions at the end of each chapter. First, the teacher has control over the questions or information presented in the study guide and can thus avoid the pitfalls of commercially developed textbook questions, which may not require the higher level thinking and responding necessary in today's fast-paced society. Second, with study guides, students don't have to wait until after they are finished reading to find out what they are expected to know, as is the case with "end-of-chapter" questions. This approach is more integrative and active from the learner's perspective, making study guides effective learning tools for students of all ages and ability levels for learning in virtually any subject or content area.

Because reading an entire selection or chapter with no assistance can be extremely labor intensive—if not impossible—for some students, especially linguistically diverse or marginalized learners, study guides are especially effective when used by students who may struggle with specific content or with comprehension in general. Study guides provide assistance without diminishing students' control over their learning because they lead them through the various information sources, guiding them to select important details and synthesize the content, often with the aid of one or more peers. As such, study guides have been called "tutors in print form" (Wood & Mateja, 1983) because they take the place of a teacher or tutor serving a printed guide through the varied sources of information. They also support assessment of instruction practices because they are a printed guide for achieving standards-based lesson objectives.

Over the years, many types of study guides have been described in the professional literature. Some guides are designed to help students recognize the patterns of text while learning content; other guides teach students how to comprehend ideas embedded in a text at different levels, from explicit to implicit; still others require that students take on the point of view of people discussed in the selection.

Evidence Supporting the Use of Study Guides

The use of study guides has long been advocated in the professional literature (Durrell, 1956; Earle, 1969; Herber, 1970; Vacca & Vacca, 2008). Nevertheless, unequivocally supporting research is limited because of the wide variation in study guides. Herber's work examines the most extensive body of research in this area (e.g., Berget, 1977; Estes, 1969; Maxon, 1979; Riley, 1979). The results of these studies indicate that study guides can be effective aids to comprehension under a variety of circumstances.

Research on the prototype of the study guide questions interspersed in text is also extensive, with studies dating back several decades (Distad, 1927; Washburne, 1929). Under the influence of behaviorism, early studies in this area used largely factual, verbatim-level questions (e.g., Frase, 1968a; Hershberger, 1964; Rothkopf, 1966). In contrast, later studies (e.g., Andre, Mueller, Womack, Smid, & Tuttle, 1980; Rickards & DiVesta, 1974), under the influence of cognitive theory, have employed higher order questions that require a greater depth of mental processing from the reader. In general, the extensive reviews of research on interspersed questions suggest that such questions tend to improve students' performance on comprehension measures (Faw & Waller, 1976; Frase, 1968b; Rickards & Denner, 1978; Rothkopf, 1966). However, these studies have received much criticism because of their contrived experimental material and preponderance of college-age subjects (MacDonald-Ross, 1978; Rickards, 1979; Tierney & Cunningham, 1984; Wood, 1986). Other research, conducted in a classroom setting with school-age subjects, has demonstrated that using interspersed questions on a variety of content area textbook selections can significantly improve students' understanding of text (Wood, 1986).

Recasting the Role of Study Guides in New Times

While study guides of all types have been used for decades to successfully aid students in content area learning and reading comprehension, study guides traditionally were applied to print-based text, usually textbooks that served as the primary information source for instruction. However, in today's classrooms, content area knowledge is no longer disseminated the way it was in previous decades. While textbooks, basal readers, and literature anthologies are still used as information sources in classrooms today, no longer are our classrooms single-textbook classrooms. Information can now be readily accessed through a wealth of multimedia and multimodal formats—so while a course textbook can certainly form a basis for instruction, it can no longer be viewed as the sole purveyor of information. Instead, information must be gained and compared from many sources. Therefore, it is necessary to recast the role of the study guide as a comprehension tool in light of these new times and new information sources.

The Influence of Multiliteracies

In today's technologically advanced society, the need for students to develop a robust understanding of discourse in all its forms is essential. As we move forward in the 21st century, there is little doubt that we will need to view text differently from the way it was viewed 50 years ago. No longer can we refer to traditional books alone as text. Now the term *text* has expanded to include print, graphic novels, art, music, digital and visual media, technical writings, popular culture such as music and television programs and characters, and Internet texts (webpages, blogs, instant messaging, for example). The list goes on and crosses grade-level boundaries. Luke and Elkins (1998) refer to this as "New Times," where reading and reading to learn are viewed as multimodal processes that involve the reading of electronic texts and the use of visual, spatial, gestural, and aural representations. Students need to develop skills to coordinate a complex set of literacy tasks, reading strategies, and language and thinking processes to negotiate a world that is becoming more and more reliant on multiple sources of information, referred to as "multiliteracies" (Cope & Kalantzis, 2000; Gee, 2004; New London Group, 1996).

Teachers can facilitate student text engagement through a variety of avenues. Popular culture can be utilized to ignite student enthusiasm. Because Western culture is saturated with media, it would be sensible to use multimedia to motivate and engage our students in reading and writing. For example, video text can be used in the classroom either singly or as a thematic compilation of excerpts (Trier, 2005). With resources such as these, we open a vista that embraces students we may have had difficulty reaching through more traditional text—while not ignoring the need to have all students connect with trade books, both narrative and informational (Duke, 2000; Harmon, Hedrick, & Wood, 2005).

Unlocking multiliteracies includes accessing, gaining, transforming, and transmitting information from text (Smith, Mikulecky, Kibby, Dreher, & Dole, 2000). As we access information, we locate text in print, oral, or visual formats. As we gain information, we use various levels of thinking skills to understand it. We transform information through written, oral, or other modes. Finally, we transmit that information as we share what we have transformed. Multiliteracies embody not just what students need to learn but how they need to learn it. Future careers for which we must prepare our students will necessitate such problem solving and creative thinking (Smith et al., 2000). Therefore, if study guides are to be used in classrooms to help students comprehend texts, study guides must be applicable and relevant to the many forms that now are considered to be texts.

The Rise of Informational Text

Often used interchangeably with the term *nonfiction* (Saul & Dieckman, 2005), informational text possesses characteristics such as factual information about the world; a more technical vocabulary; definitional content; and visuals such as maps, graphs, and charts (Duke, 2000; Duke & Kays, 1998). Informational text can have specific structural elements such as compare/contrast, problem/solution, and cause/effect as well as more global elements, including an introduction, descriptions, characteristics of the topic, processes or events, and a brief summary (Pappas, 1986).

With the expansion and accessibility of multiple sources of information, students are constantly bombarded with choices of informational texts. As the key to accessing knowledge in society, student success in our classrooms today and in their careers tomorrow mandates that they be proficient in navigating informational text (Duke, 2000). Even as we recognize this, we must also acknowledge that classrooms have not always been successful in preparing students to read and write a wide array of informational texts. Since the enactment of No Child Left Behind legislation in the United States, increased attention has been placed on student testing of information contained in nonnarrative formats (Saul & Dieckman, 2005). To accommodate this schools have integrated greater amounts of informational text reading in the curriculum, and teachers have sought support to become more skillful in designing instruction that enables students to successfully interact with informational text reading.

One approach that has strengthened these advances in instruction has been to support content area teaching with literacy instruction. This has mutually enhanced both content and literacy learning (Palincsar & Duke, 2004). For example, as students debate ideas and make connections about information found in content texts, their knowledge base and thinking are enhanced (Pappas & Varelas, 2004). Therefore, study guides must offer a means to help students make these connections, determine the most important information, and engage in what Allington (2006) calls "thoughtful literacy." The guides offered in this book—strategy guides, rather than study guides—enable students to do this.

Moving From Study Guides to Strategy Guides

To reflect changes in the field of literacy over the past several decades and the new definitions of what constitutes *text*, the guides in this book utilize a multiliteracies perspective and draw on far more sources of information than the single textbook approach of previous decades. In addition, we have renamed the study guides featured in this book "strategy guides" and likewise created or revised these guides to reflect what their name suggests. This name change is supported by an understanding in the field of literacy about what constitutes sources of learning. Unlike traditional study guides, the strategy guides in this book represent the expanded view of information sources. This expanded view has resulted in less reliance on a single text—most often the textbook—in the content areas to many sources and forms of information as a means of expanding students' depth of knowledge about the topic under study. The strategy guides provide a vehicle to access and scaffold information from a wide range of texts including print texts, those electronically accessed on the Internet or via a website, and even other information sources that may be less tactile, such as information offered through field trips, artifacts, united streaming video, or class experiments.

Strategy guides then derive their name from the concept that the end goal of effective instruction is the creation of independent, strategic learners. This instruction starts with the teacher; is scaffolded, guided, and expanded via the strategy guide activities and questions; and then concludes with students who emerge more metacognitively aware of how to gain information from multiple sources of content. As the information sources encountered become more diverse, the more strategies and strategizing students must employ to determine the most significant content. The activities and questions developed for the guides are just as important as the teacher modeling, explanation, and thinking aloud that coincides with their introduction. Equally significant in this strategic process is the peer interaction and socially constructed knowledge that take place as students share their thinking with and learn from one another; we discuss this in greater detail in the section that follows.

Figure 1 is adapted from a study guide excerpt that appeared in the first edition of this book (Wood, Lapp, & Flood, 1992) and illustrates how some of the questions and activities asked in a traditional guide can be

Figure 1. Example of Traditional Guide Questions Used With Multiple Sources

Natural Resources

Source	Topic/Heading	Task: Question or Activity
p. 275	Riches of the Earth	What are our natural resources? In your own words, tell why they are important.
pp. 275–6	Forests	Discuss three facts you have learned from reading this section.
Website	www.nrcs.usda.gov/	Briefly explain programs available for conserving our forests. Discuss with your partner what you can do to conserve our forests.
p. 275	Graph on Fuels	What does this graph tell you about which area produces the most crude oil each year? What are the implications of this information?

Adapted from Wood, K.D., Lapp, D., & Flood, J. (1992). *Guiding readers through text: A review of study guides* (p. 1). Newark, DE: International Reading Association.

expanded to include multiple sources for additional, updated information. This example illustrates the basic study guide format based on a text chapter while also leading students to alternative sources of information, in this case a website on natural resources. Notice how this guide helps focus students' attention on the graphic aids in the printed material, which are typically overlooked by most readers.

The Extended Anticipation Guide (see page 95) is another example of a strategy guide's adaptability for use with alternative texts. The traditional Anticipation Guide (see page 89) includes a series of approximately 5 to 10 statements to which students respond before reading, use as a guide during reading, and then return to after the reading for discussion, synthesis, and reflection. In the figure on page 99, a secondary-level history teacher has designed an Extended Anticipation Guide on the riots in Tiananmen Square in China that requires students to visit websites, Wikipedia (the online encyclopedia) entries, and other electronic texts to discover the answers.

Strategy Guides as Vehicles for Socially Constructed Knowledge

Based on the theories of Vygotsky (1934/1978), the idea of scaffolding involves the zone of proximal development (ZPD) where students learn with the assistance of a more proficient peer, teacher, or tutor. Therefore, scaffolding is typically social in nature. This theoretical zone exists between a student's ability to be independently successful and to be successful with expert help and results in increased opportunities to grow into an autonomous reader and writer (Beed, Hawkins, & Roller, 1991). On their way to developing this autonomy, students are cognitively supported in addition to receiving motivational and emotional support (Meyer & Turner, 2002), or as Yowell and Smylie (1999) state, "There develops a common understanding between learner and teacher to bridge the distance between expert and novice" (p. 474).

Strategy guides also serve as vehicles for socially constructed knowledge due to the social interaction that is included in the design of the strategy guides and their corresponding activities. In the General Guidelines for Classroom Use section in chapter 2 (see pages 24–27) we recommend that students be allowed to work together to complete them. Some guides are specifically designed with the collaborative element, such as the Collaborative Guides in Part II of this book. These guides require students to work in preassigned heterogeneous groups and pairs. However, we recommend that teachers consider allowing students to work in pairs or small groups to complete *all* of the guides included in this book. The power of socially constructed knowledge is well documented in the literature. From a theoretical perspective, learning is a social process (Luria, 1976; Vygotsky, 1934/1978). From an empirical perspective, there is more evidence for the benefits of collaborative learning than any other aspect of education (Johnson & Johnson, 1985). Further, the strategy guides used for any given lesson can be designed with creativity to entice students to participate in the learning process, and students are also further motivated to participate because the mere act of discussing ideas with a partner is often encouragement enough for students to attend to and complete a task.

The Role of Strategy Guides in the Development of Strategic Readers

The end goal of any instruction, including the use of strategy guides, is the development of independent, strategic readers and writers. In order to become strategic, students need guidance, modeling, and assistance in the form of scaffolded instruction. Scaffolded instruction can take various forms. Instructional practices such as modeling and remodeling, questioning, teacher feedback, clarification, misconception correction, and using analogies are common variations (Many, 2002).

Scaffolding is accomplished in the context of models of teacher-directed instruction, of which there are many in the professional literature (Clark & Graves, 2005; Paris, Lipson, & Wixson, 1983). For example, Pearson and Gallagher (1983) propose a graduated release model that follows a continuum from the teacher "taking all or most of the responsibility for task completion" via the use of modeling comprehension techniques to, ultimately, the student taking the responsibility while practicing or applying strategy.

Strategy guides by design are vehicles for providing the scaffolding necessary for helping students understand extended print and nonprint discourse. We envision strategy guides as using the gradual release model but with the added social support necessary for shared knowledge and authentic learning. Therefore, we use a Phased Transfer Model of Instruction with flexible grouping (Wood, 2002; Wood & Taylor, 2006). Figure 2 is a generic illustration of how that model can be applied to the use of strategy guides. The Phased Transfer Model acknowledges that teaching and learning are discursive and transactional in nature. That is, teaching and learning occur in a social environment in which students work both individually and in groups and in which teachers play different roles of involvement. The Phased Transfer Model is one way of explaining that complex set of transactions.

The Phased Transfer Model suggests multiple uses for strategy guides that can move from more teacher-centered to student-centered groupings of students. From the initial teacher explanation of the purposes of the guide and demonstrations of its use, the students begin to work together in preassigned pairs or groups to take the responsibility for their own learning.

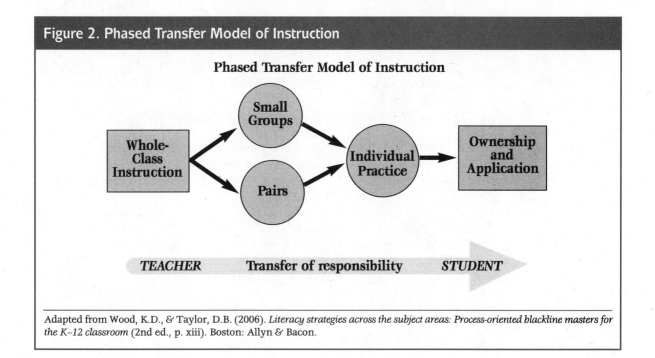

Figure 2. Phased Transfer Model of Instruction

Adapted from Wood, K.D., & Taylor, D.B. (2006). *Literacy strategies across the subject areas: Process-oriented blackline masters for the K–12 classroom* (2nd ed., p. xiii). Boston: Allyn & Bacon.

As you prepare to implement strategy guides in your classroom, keep in mind that strategy guides are only a stepping stone to independent learning. Once students have mastered a learning strategy using a guide, it is important to teach them how to apply that strategy on their own. A major goal of strategy guides is to make their use obsolete by creating more reflective and metacognitive learners.

REFERENCES

Allington, R.L. (2006). *What really matters for struggling readers: Designing research-based programs* (2nd ed.). Boston: Allyn & Bacon.

Alvermann, D.E., & Phelps, S.F. (2001). *Content reading and literacy: Succeeding in today's diverse classrooms* (3rd ed.). Boston: Allyn & Bacon.

Andre, T., Mueller, C., Womack, S., Smid, K., & Tuttle, M. (1980). Adjunct application questions facilitate later application—or do they? *Journal of Educational Psychology, 72,* 533–543.

Anstey, M., & Bull, G. (2006). *Teaching and learning multiliteracies: Changing times, changing literacies.* Newark, DE: International Reading Association.

Beed, P.L., Hawkins, E.M., & Roller, C.M. (1991). Moving learners toward independence: The power of scaffolded instruction. *The Reading Teacher, 44,* 648–655.

Berget, E. (1977). The use of organizational pattern guides, structured overviews, and visual summaries in guiding social studies reading. In H.L. Herber & R.T. Vacca (Eds.), *Research in reading in the content areas: The third report* (pp. 151–162). Syracuse, NY: Syracuse University Reading and Language Arts Center.

Clark, K.F., & Graves, M.F. (2005). Scaffolding students' comprehension of text. *The Reading Teacher, 58,* 570–580.

Cope, B., & Kalantzis, M. (Eds.). (2000). *Multiliteracies: Literacy learning and the design of social futures.* New York: Routledge.

Distad, H.W. (1927). A study of the reading performance of pupils under different conditions on different types of materials. *Journal of Educational Psychology, 18,* 247–258.

Duke, N.K. (2000). 3.6 minutes per day: The scarcity of informational texts in first grade. *Reading Research Quarterly, 35,* 202–224.

Duke, N.K., & Kays, J. (1998). "Can I say 'Once upon a time'?" Kindergarten children developing knowledge of information book language. *Early Childhood Research Quarterly, 13,* 295–318.

Durrell, D.D. (1956). *Improving reading instruction.* Yonkers-on-Hudson, NY: World Book.

Earle, R.A. (1969). Use of the structured overview in mathematics classes. In H.L. Herber & P.L. Sanders (Eds.), *Research in reading in the content areas: First year report* (pp. 49–58). Syracuse, NY: Syracuse University Reading and Language Arts Center.

Estes, T.H. (1969). Use of prepared guide material and small group discussion in reading ninth grade social studies assignments. In H.L. Herber & P.L. Sanders (Eds.), *Research in reading in the content areas: First year report* (pp. 64–70). Syracuse, NY: Syracuse University Reading and Language Arts Center.

Faw, H.W., & Waller, T.G. (1976). Mathemagenic behaviors and efficiency in learning from prose materials: Review, critique, and recommendations. *Review of Educational Research, 46,* 691–720.

Frase, L.T. (1968a). Effect of question location, pacing, and mode upon retention of prose material. *Journal of Educational Psychology, 59,* 244–249.

Frase, L.T. (1968b). Questions as aids to reading: Some research and theory. *American Education Research Journal, 5*, 319–332.

Gee, J.P. (2004). *Situated language and learning: A critique of traditional schooling.* New York: Routledge.

Harmon, J.M., Hedrick, W.B., & Wood, K.D. (2005). Research on vocabulary instruction in the content areas: Implications for struggling readers. *Reading and Writing Quarterly, 21*, 261–280.

Herber, H.L. (1970). *Teaching reading in the content areas.* Upper Saddle River, NJ: Prentice Hall.

Hershberger, W. (1964). Self-evaluational responding and typographical cueing: Techniques for programming self-instructional reading materials. *Journal of Educational Psychology, 55*, 288–296.

Johnson, R.T., & Johnson, D.W. (1985). Student-student interaction: Ignored but powerful. *Journal of Teacher Education, 36*(4), 22–26.

Karchmer, R.A., Mallette, M.H., Kara-Soteriou, J., & Leu, D.J. (Eds.). (2005). *Innovative approaches to literacy education: Using the Internet to support new literacies.* Newark, DE: International Reading Association.

Lapp, D., Flood, J., & Farnan, N. (2007). *Content area reading & learning: Instructional strategies* (3rd ed.). Mahwah, NJ: Erlbaum.

Luke, A., & Elkins, J. (1998). Reinventing literacy in "New Times." *Journal of Adolescent & Adult Literacy, 42*, 4–7.

Luria, A.R. (1976). *Cognitive development: Its cultural and social foundations.* Cambridge, MA: Harvard University Press.

MacDonald-Ross, M. (1978). Language in texts: The design of curricular materials. *Review of Research in Education, 6*, 229–275.

Many, J.E. (2002). An exhibition and analysis of verbal tapestries: Understanding how scaffolding is woven into the fabric of instructional conversations. *Reading Research Quarterly, 37*, 376–407.

Manzo, A.V., Manzo, U.C., & Thomas, M.M. (2004). *Content area literacy: Strategic thinking for strategic learning* (4th ed.). New York: Wiley.

Maxon, G.A. (1979). An investigation of the relative effect between questions and declarative statements as guides to reading comprehension for seventh grade students. In H.L. Herber & J.D. Riley (Eds.), *Research in reading in the content areas: The fourth report* (pp. 66–78). Syracuse, NY: Syracuse University Reading and Language Arts Center.

Meyer, D.K., & Turner, J.C. (2002). Using instructional discourse analysis to study the scaffolding of student self-regulation. *Educational Psychologist, 37*, 17–25.

New London Group. (1996). A pedagogy of multiliteracies: Designing social futures. *Harvard Educational Review, 66*, 60–92.

Palincsar, A.S., & Duke, N.K. (2004). The role of text and text-reader interactions in young children's reading development and achievement. *The Elementary School Journal, 105*, 183–197.

Pappas, C.C. (1986, December). *Exploring the global structure of "information books."* Paper presented at the 36th annual meeting of the National Reading Conference, Austin, TX. (ERIC Document Reproduction Service No. ED298952)

Pappas, C.C., & Varelas, M. (with Barry, A., & Rife, A.). (2004). Promoting dialogic inquiry in information book read-alouds: Young urban children's ways of making sense in science. In E.W. Saul (Ed.), *Crossing borders in literacy and science instruction: Perspectives on theory and practice* (pp. 161–189). Newark, DE: International Reading Association; Arlington, VA: National Science Teachers Association.

Paris, S.G., Lipson, M.Y., & Wixson, K.K. (1983). Becoming a strategic reader. *Contemporary Educational Psychology, 8*, 293–316.

Pearson, P.D., & Gallagher, M.C. (1983). The instruction of reading comprehension. *Contemporary Educational Psychology, 8,* 317–344.

Rickards, J.P. (1979). Adjunct postquestions in text: A critical review of methods and processes. *Review of Educational Research, 49,* 181–196.

Rickards, J.P., & Denner, P.R. (1978). Inserted questions as aids to reading text. *Instructional Science, 7,* 313–346.

Rickards, J.P., & DiVesta, F.J. (1974). Type and frequency of questions in processing textual materials. *Journal of Educational Psychology, 66,* 354–362.

Riley, J.D. (1979). The effects of reading guides and a directed reading method on word problem comprehension, problem solving ability, and attitude towards mathematics. In H.L. Herber & J.D. Riley (Eds.), *Research in reading in the content areas: The fourth report* (pp. 79–98). Syracuse, NY: Syracuse University Reading and Language Arts Center.

Rothkopf, E.Z. (1966). Learning from written instructive materials: An explanation of the control of inspection behavior by test-like events. *American Educational Research Journal, 3,* 241–249.

Saul, E.W., & Dieckman, D. (2005). Choosing and using information trade books. *Reading Research Quarterly, 40,* 502–513.

Smith, M.C., Mikulecky, L., Kibby, M.W., Dreher, M.J., & Dole, J.A. (2000). What will be the demands of literacy in the workplace in the next millennium? *Reading Research Quarterly, 35,* 378–383.

Tierney, R.J., & Cunningham, J.W. (1984). Research on teaching reading comprehension. In P.D. Pearson, R. Barr, M.L. Kamil, & P. Mosenthal (Eds.), *Handbook of reading research* (pp. 609–656). New York: Longman.

Trier, J. (2005). Pedagogy of the obsessed. *Journal of Adolescent & Adult Literacy, 49,* 238–241.

Vacca, R.T., & Vacca, J.A.L. (2008). *Content area reading: Literacy and learning across the curriculum* (9th ed.). Boston: Allyn & Bacon.

Vygotsky, L.S. (1978). *Mind in society: The development of higher psychological processes* (M. Cole, V. John-Steiner, S. Scribner, & E. Souberman, Eds. & Trans.). Cambridge, MA: Harvard University Press. (Original work published 1934)

Washburne, J.N. (1929). The use of questions in social science material. *Journal of Educational Psychology, 20,* 321–359.

Wood, K.D. (1986). The effect of interspersing questions in text: Evidence for "slicing the task." *Reading Research and Instruction, 25,* 295–307.

Wood, K.D. (2002). Differentiating reading and writing lessons to promote content learning. In C.C. Block, L.B. Gambrell, & M. Pressley (Eds.), *Improving comprehension instruction: Rethinking research, theory, and classroom practice* (pp. 155–180). San Francisco: Jossey-Bass; Newark, DE: International Reading Association.

Wood, K.D., Lapp, D., & Flood, J. (1992). *Guiding readers through text: A review of study guides.* Newark, DE: International Reading Association.

Wood, K.D., & Mateja, J.A. (1983). Adapting secondary level strategies for use in elementary classrooms. *The Reading Teacher, 36,* 492–496.

Wood, K.D., & Taylor, D.B. (2006). *Literacy strategies across the subject areas: Process-oriented blackline masters for the K–12 classroom* (2nd ed.). Boston: Allyn & Bacon.

Yowell, C.M., & Smylie, M.A. (1999). Self-regulation in democratic communities. *The Elementary School Journal, 99,* 469–490.

CHAPTER 2

Getting Started With Strategy Guides

In today's technologically advanced world, teachers and students have more sources of information available than ever before. Finding ways to consolidate these sources in a meaningful and manageable way can be challenging. That is where the strategy guide can become an invaluable resource. Strategy guides can take the place of the teacher by directing students to multiple sources on a topic under study while simultaneously guiding them to the most significant content. They are a vehicle for integrating effective literacy skills across the subject areas, providing students with a scaffold to independent and strategic reading and learning. Strategy guides help students to focus on what is important, leading them to not simply read text, but to also actively interact with the content, making analogies, connecting to their prior knowledge and experiences, and critically analyzing the author's message. Strategy guides help them see what to focus on, what to skim, and what to skip over while reading and attending to information.

Unfortunately, when some teachers and students think of traditional study guides, their experiences may not always have been positive ones. Guides are not designed to be completed in isolation. They are not tests, nor are they fill-in-the-blank worksheets to be handed to students without guidance or peer or teacher assistance. They gain their benefits through the social dimension, requiring much student-to-student and student-to-teacher discussion and interaction.

However, strategy guides, when used effectively, do as their name suggests. They guide students' reading and comprehension strategy use before, during, and after a lesson. Therefore, to get the most benefit from

Guiding Readers Through Text: Strategy Guides for New Times (2nd ed.) by Karen D. Wood, Diane Lapp, James Flood, and D. Bruce Taylor. © 2008 by the International Reading Association.

strategy guides, teachers must know how to choose and use the most appropriate guide for a given learning situation. This chapter shows you how to do this, how to decide whether a guide is needed in the learning experience by analyzing the materials and student needs, and how to move forward to match the guide to those materials and student needs. The chapter also illustrates how to model the use of strategy guides with your students and provides classroom guidelines for the use of strategy guides.

How to Select a Strategy Guide

Every teacher has known the frustration of trying to meet the needs of a class full of students with diverse ability levels. In a collaborative group, students' reading proficiencies will vary widely. This variance becomes more pronounced as students move up the grade levels. For example, a 10th-grade classroom may have a 10-year span of performance that ranges from the 5th-grade level or lower to the college level (Singer & Donlan, 1989). While the single-textbook classroom is and should be an artifact of the past, textbooks are still in use in today's classrooms as at least one source of information or, in some cases, the primary or core source. Many of these textbooks are what Armbruster (2007) calls "inconsiderate"—that is, they are difficult to understand and assume too much knowledge on the part of the reader. With such a wide range of performance in a given classroom and the inconsiderate nature of traditional text, it is not surprising that many students will have difficulty reading and comprehending the grade-level text.

Strategy guides can be a great help to teachers, but only when chosen and used with care. The following guidelines will help you first to determine whether a strategy guide is the most appropriate instructional tool for a given situation and then to decide which one to use.

Decide Whether a Guide Is Needed

Before determining how to teach a particular body of information, you must first decide what you plan to teach about the particular topic. Ask yourself the following questions:

- What concepts do I want my students to know after reading the material?
- Which vocabulary terms are essential to understand these concepts?
- Does the text include important dates, numbers, or other data that students should know?
- Which subtopics will require more emphasis?

The next step is to determine whether a chapter or other segment of text warrants the use of a strategy guide, given the information you want students to learn. Often a teacher will have noted the previous year that the students found one or more chapters of a textbook particularly challenging. They may have been unable to recall or discuss major concepts from those chapters, or their responses may have sounded very literal or "textbook-like," indicating that they had not integrated the new information with their preexisting knowledge. In other instances, the teacher realizes on previewing a text selection that, while the content is integral to the lesson objectives, the style, concept load, or mode of presentation is just too overwhelming for independent reading. Help is then needed, particularly for struggling or below grade-level readers. That help can take the form of a strategy guide.

It's important to remember that a guide can do only so much. For example, a strategy guide for a chapter on Japan may focus students' attention on descriptions of topography, industry, people, and other important topics, as well as help students connect that information to their prior knowledge by having them brainstorm what they already know. However, you may feel that a video, Podcast, united streaming on the customs of Japan, an outside speaker, or simply more teacher-led discussion would be helpful as well. Therefore, do not rely on a strategy guide as the sole purveyor of content area information (just as textbooks should not be relied on as the sole purveyor of information, as discussed in chapter 1). But in combination with your own knowledge, as well as other sources of information, strategy guides can be powerful instructional tools.

Analyze the Material and Student Needs

Once you've determined that a strategy guide is beneficial, the next step is to analyze the material to note its salient features. We have presented some of the questions and concerns teachers would ask in the form of a checklist shown in Figure 3 (see page 174 in the Appendix for a reproducible version of this checklist). The checklist is filled out for an intermediate-level lesson in science on the topic of arthropods. As a result of this analysis, the teacher decided to develop a Reading Road Map on the lesson (see chapter 21, Figure 52). While completing a checklist for every lesson would be too time-consuming, it can serve as an aid, a thinking tool, to help teachers decide how to proceed when a lesson requires additional external guidance and support. In order to determine the demands of the text or any information source, ask yourself some of the following questions:

- Is the text fiction or nonfiction?
- Is the primary text pattern cause and effect, main idea and supporting details, or a sequence?

Figure 3. Teacher Checklist for Evaluating a Text

Evaluating the Text	YES	NO
Fiction		*No*
Nonfiction	*Science*	
Cause/Effect		*No*
Descriptive/Definitions	*Tells about types of arthropods*	
Compare/Contrast	*a few instances*	
Sequential		*Yes, website on evolution especially*
Problem/Solution		*No*
Are related concepts introduced within a few pages?	*Throughout text*	
Can portions of the selection be skipped?	*Yes, at least skimmed*	
Do some portions or sources require more thorough reading?	*Yes, new concepts and many descriptions*	
Are other sources of information needed?	*Yes, website on evolution of arthropods*	

- Are there a lot of related concepts?
- Are the explanations somewhat sketchy and difficult to understand?

As you scrutinize the text, these questions and more will begin to surface; their answers will help you decide how the content may best be conveyed.

In concert with this step, you should begin to consider what skills and strategies the reader will need to comprehend the material. Ask yourself the following questions:

- Does the text contain gaps that require much inferencing?
- Are there a lot of facts that students need to learn?
- Do I need to model and teach inferential or evaluative thinking to ensure a thorough understanding?
- Is it important that the reader be able to distinguish main ideas from details?

Figure 4. Teacher Checklist for Evaluating the Reader		
Evaluating the Reader— Reader needs support to:	**YES**	**NO**
Identify basic, explicitly stated ideas and/or details	Yes, Many details and descriptions	
Understand author intent		No
Identify propositions		No
Identify descriptive words and phrases to support visualization	Yes	
Connect personal experiences with author clues to make inferences	Somewhat	
Identify and use major elements to synthesize the text	Yes	
Use collected inferences and personal insights to evaluate the major premise		No, Mostly requiring literal understanding
Summarize by scaffolding major ideas	Yes	
Take a critical stance		No

- Will students benefit particularly from being able to adjust their rate of reading for this selection?
- Will the students be more motivated to read the selection if they assume the perspective of the main character?
- Will they learn best by working individually, in small groups, or with the whole class?

Your answers can be compiled in a chart similar to the one shown in Figure 4 (see page 175 in the Appendix for a reproducible version of this checklist).

Match the Guide to the Material and the Reader Needs

After completing these charts you will know what content you want to teach, what the features of the reading material are, and what strategies students will need to understand that material. You will also know that a strategy guide is needed to convey the content effectively. Now it's time to decide which guide best fits your overall lesson objectives.

For this phase in the decision-making process, we will use a specific example. Let's suppose that you are teaching an eighth-grade lesson on radioactivity and the next chapter segment deals with detecting radiation.

You know that many of your students have had difficulty comprehending the previous chapters, and you decide that giving them some instruction in how to read their science text may help them not only with this chapter but with others as well.

Looking ahead, you see that the next several chapters contain many cause-and-effect passages. Taking this into account along with your lesson objectives, you'd probably select the Process Guide (described fully in chapter 20) because it has an extensive modeling component and is designed to introduce the notion of text structure. Specifically, the Process Guide takes the students through an entire lesson, beginning with the modeling of the skill or process (e.g., cause and effect, summarizing, sequencing, drawing conclusions, predicting outcomes, locating the main idea) and moving on to examples for whole-class use and practice items for small groups or pairs. After working through this initial teaching portion of the guide, students can apply these skills and processes to the textbook selection.

In subsequent reading assignments in science, you can reinforce students' understanding of the cause-and-effect relationship by drawing their attention to relevant patterns of text and eliciting their input. You may also want to describe how this process can be applied in other subject areas.

The Process-of-Reading Guide is well suited to this particular instructional situation and can be adapted to your specific needs. In a different situation—say, if you wanted to focus on the compare-and-contrast structure—another type of study guide might be more effective. The detailed descriptions in Table 1 should give you the information you need to make the most appropriate choice at any given time. This chart outlines the various types of strategy guides described in this book and a brief summary of the primary objectives of each to help in your selection. As you can see, there is a broad array from which to choose. Later sections, which describe each type of guide in detail, provide more specifics about their appropriateness for different class sizes, subject areas, and grade levels. We have found that many guides can be adapted across most or all of these areas. Of course, you should use your own ideas and creativity in modifying them for your students.

After familiarizing yourself with the strategy guides described in this book, use this chart to help match your lesson objectives with the most appropriate guide. The chart provides the page number of each guide's full description.

Modeling the Use of Strategy Guides

The primary goal of using a strategy guide is enabling your students to become independent, strategic readers. To aid them in doing so, it is

Table 1. Outline of Strategy Guides, Primary Objectives, and Features

Guide	Primary Objectives and Features	Page
COLLABORATIVE GUIDES	**Guides in this section are designed to foster discussion and require group interaction.**	
Collaborative Listening–Viewing Guide	Uses peer interaction to solidify students' understanding and recall of information heard or viewed.	31
Interactive Reading Guide	Promotes peer interaction through discussion, retelling, brainstorming, and other activities.	37
Reciprocal Teaching Discussion Guide	Helps students share their thinking and work in groups to predict, clarify, summarize, question.	45
THINKING GUIDES	**These guides help students analyze, interpret, question, and synthesize information from varied sources and engage in critical thinking.**	
Critical Profiler Guide	Uses questions to assist students in taking a critical stance while reading to question authors' purposes.	53
Inquiry Guide	Helps students organize and seek out information from varied sources to answer questions about text.	61
Learning-From-Text Guide	Helps students understand literal, inferential, and evaluative levels of information.	65
Multiple-Source Research Guide	Helps students work collaboratively to summarize research from varied sources and write a synthesis.	73
Point-of-View Guide	Broadens perspective by making use of elaboration and prior knowledge.	77
STATEMENT GUIDES	**Guides in this section give teachers the opportunity to witness cognitive growth. They see where students are in their thinking in the prereading stage, and they get to eavesdrop on students' new learning, as reflected in discussions, during the postreading stage.**	
Anticipation Guide	Activates students' prior knowledge and stimulates discussion before and after reading or viewing.	89
Extended Anticipation Guide	Activates students' prior knowledge and justifies reactions to content in writing.	95
Reaction Review Guide	Reviews concepts, solidifies understanding, and incorporates written justification, especially for mathematics.	101
MANIPULATIVE GUIDES	**Guides in this section provide students with physical tools for organizing and thinking about content and are especially motivating and interesting for diverse learners and student proficiencies.**	
Foldable Guide	Organizes content in a physical, tactile way.	107
Origami Guide	Organizes content in a 3-D format.	115

(continued)

Guide	Primary Objectives and Features	Page
TEXT STRUCTURE GUIDES	**These guides help students organize their thinking to coordinate with the varied text structures they will encounter while reading from multiple text sources.**	
Analogical Study Guide	Extends students' comprehension and recall of main concepts through the use of analogies.	123
Concept Guide	Helps students understand the function of main ideas and supporting details through categorization.	131
Pattern Guide	Helps students understand various organizational patterns of text (e.g., cause and effect, sequencing, compare and contrast).	137
PROCESSES-OF-READING GUIDES	**Guides in this section help students simulate the reading process by employing metacognitive skills and strategies.**	
Glossing	Directs students' attention to text features (figures of speech, concepts, contrasts, main ideas) and helps them develop strategies (using context, predicting, drawing conclusions) through the use of marginal notations.	145
Process Guide	Teaches various processes involved in reading (e.g., drawing conclusions, predicting outcomes, identifying the main idea, sequencing).	151
Reading Road Map	Helps students develop flexibility in reading rate.	155
Textbook Activity Guide	Helps students monitor their comprehension through predicting, retelling, and outlining.	161
TRANSFERRING TO INDEPENDENT LEARNING		
Student-Developed Guide	Releases responsibility to students for developing their own guide for reading when less teacher guidance is needed.	167

important to model for them how any guide can be used independently to support their comprehension. Ample research attests to the value of modeling skills and strategies before assigning independent practice (Berliner & Rosenshine, 1977; Duffy & McIntyre, 1982; Methe & Hintze, 2003). It is essential that you, the teacher, thoroughly explain the purpose of the reading guides and "walk and talk" students through the assignment. This helps students gain a metacognitive understanding of why such guides can help them learn. The following section offers our recommended procedure for modeling the use of strategy guides.

Explain the Purpose of the Guide

Tell the students that the guide is used to do just what its name suggests: to guide them through text material and help them determine the most significant content. Begin by asking, "How many of you would like help understanding and remembering what you read? How many of you would like help picking out the most important information from your text, a website, an online encyclopedia entry?" Hands will go up because you will have captured students' interest and sparked their motivation.

Preview the Guide

Hand out the guide you have selected to the students and go over the organization, showing them how the guide coordinates with the text or other content sources from which the questions and activities are drawn. Explain to your students that this previewing gives them an overview of what to read in depth and what can be skipped or skimmed. This is important information to a reader. Tell them that, while they are using a printed guide now, the end goal is for them to be able to read information and reflect on and pick out what is significant on their own.

Modeling and Think-Aloud Sample Responses

Walk the students through one or more of the items on the guide, thinking aloud your responses. Be sure to explain to the students why you focused on certain information and eliminated other content. Take the opportunity to tell them how valuable it is to take on a reading selection one paragraph or "chunk" at a time, just as the guide is "telling" them to do.

Release the Responsibility to Groups or Pairs

Now it is time to let the students try a few items in pairs or small groups, reading a portion of the text and then "talking aloud" their responses to one another. While this is going on, be sure to circulate, monitor, and assist the students. Sometimes it is necessary to go back and revisit the whole-class, think-aloud step described previously with groups or even the whole class when students are still having difficulty.

Release the Responsibility to the Individual

When you feel that the students grasp the concept of the guide you have developed, allow them to proceed on their own or in pairs. We like the idea of letting students work together even at this stage because of the value of sharing knowledge and talking about what they are reading and learning, but the choice is yours to make. Again you should monitor and confer with individuals to determine if extra support is needed.

Incorporate a Discussion of Responses

We strongly encourage discussion throughout the entire process. You may choose to allow students to have small-group, paired, or whole-class discussions after completing a few items or wait until the guide is finished. Tell them how important it is to talk about the content, retell, and put the information in their own words. Explain that even talking to themselves either mentally or subvocally will help them remember and recall information when they are reading on their own without a guide. We suggest reminding them to read in segments and after each segment of content to ask themselves "What did I just read? Can I say it in my own words?"

Have the Students Develop a Guide

After you feel they have had sufficient practice with the teacher-prepared guide concept, you may want to have students develop a guide on their own. This is illustrated in more detail in the Student-Developed Guide description in chapter 23 of this book.

Have the Students Illustrate Independent Application of Strategies

Now it is time to have the students read another selection, this time applying the same strategies on their own with no guide present. Then, continue to encourage them in subsequent reading of related assignments to use strategies such as "chunking" their reading, skimming over less important information, and restating the information in their own words after reading. Their success at this point signifies their independence as readers who effectively comprehend the texts they encounter.

General Guidelines for Classroom Use

To aid you in implementing strategy guides that support your students as they acquire the knowledge needed to comprehend texts and analyze the topics presented in them, we offer the following guidelines and recommendations. As with any instructional strategy, you will need to adapt your approach to take into account the students' prior knowledge, the demands of the text and other information sources, and your lesson standards and objectives. However, these general guidelines should help in most situations.

Encourage Higher Order Thinking

A well-designed guide should have increasingly complex questions and activities to support and scaffold higher order thinking skills. The strategy guides included in this book are designed to support readers as they develop complex thinking and language processes through questions and experiences that engage them in literal, interpretative, and evaluative thinking, and any guide you use in your classroom should offer similar experiences.

Design Engaging Guides

The more creative the guide is in appearance and content, the more likely it is that students will want to read the assigned text. A guide on the cardiovascular system, for example, may take the shape of a heart with questions or activities marking significant locations. Guide questions and activities should likewise be designed to stimulate creative thinking and student engagement.

Incorporate Multiple Sources of Information Where Appropriate

While it may be necessary and useful to develop guides for a single source of information, in today's technologically changing world, guide activities and questions can lead students to other sources of information to deepen their understanding and broaden their view.

Adapt the Instruction for English-Language Learners and Other Diverse Learners

We have included a section at the conclusion of each guide chapter called Tips for Diverse Learners. These suggestions are for students for whom English is a second language and for any other students with diverse needs and requiring additional assistance. Many of the tips involve the use of research-proven approaches for English-language learners such as including collaborative learning, getting English-proficient or more reading proficient students to help and tutor those in need, using visual aids and pictures to illustrate concepts, and preteaching, emphasizing, and reviewing significant terms (Hill & Flynn, 2006; Wood & Beattie, 2004; Wood & Tinajero, 2002).

Build in a Review of the Content

Frequent review of information learned improves long-term understanding and retention (Alvermann & Phelps, 2005; Good & Grouws, 1979). The culminating activity of a study guide should involve a mental and written review of the major concepts, events, or people discussed in the text. Ask students to associate the new information with their prior knowledge and to recall all they can while the information is still readily accessible.

Encourage Skimming/Previewing Before Beginning

Skimming and previewing the guide and the text before beginning should become automatic for students after the initial instruction and modeling. This helps students solidify their purpose for reading and allows them to see where they are going before they get there.

Group and Pair Students

The Collaborative Guides in Part II of this book are designed specifically to capitalize on the many advantages of cooperative learning, but all reading guides should have some element of student-to-student and student-to-teacher interaction. Such collaboration not only improves achievement but also greatly enhances relationships among students (Johnson & Johnson, 1985; Totten, Sills, Digby, & Russ, 1991).

Circulate and Monitor

The most effective teachers continually circulate and monitor class assignments (Evertson, Emmer, & Clements, 1984; Kelley & Clausen-Grace, 2006; Kounin, 1970). This level of involvement in the lesson allows you to assist individuals or groups and to determine who may need further encouragement.

Include Frequent Class Discussion During Use

Strategy guides require teacher direction to be effective. Their value diminishes when students are told merely to turn in their assignment when finished. Follow-up discussions of students' guide responses are essential with each lesson to increase interest, learning, and later recall. You can also encourage group or whole-class discussion at certain junctures as a way to review the learning and clear up any potential misconceptions early in the reading.

Use Strategy Guides Judiciously

Strategy guides should not be designed for every chapter or text selection. As with any strategy, their novelty would soon wear off and their utility would diminish. Use of guides should be limited to portions of the text that may be difficult for students to follow or that are particularly suitable for such treatment.

Avoid Assigning Grades

Strategy guides are aids developed to assist students with classroom material and various types of texts. Therefore, they should not be graded in the competitive sense, particularly because the finished guides are often the result of a group effort. Group members should be given either a "complete" or an "incomplete," if any grade at all.

Encourage Strategic Reading

Strategic readers read purposefully and with direction, and they know what to do when something fails to make sense. In short, they know what strategies to use and when to use them (Bishop, Reyes, & Pflaum, 2006; Frey, 2006; Paris, Lipson, & Wixson, 1983; Vacca & Vacca, 2008). Strategy guides are a means of making students aware of the range of strategies necessary for successful comprehension. It is essential to explain how these strategies apply to other contexts (both within and outside of the classroom) and how they can be employed independently when no guide is available.

REFERENCES

Alvermann, D.E., & Phelps, S.F. (2005). *Content reading and literacy: Succeeding in today's diverse classrooms* (4th ed.). Boston: Allyn & Bacon.

Armbruster, B. (2007). Matching readers and texts: The continuing quest. In D. Lapp, J. Flood, & N. Farnan (Eds.), *Content area reading and learning: Instructional strategies* (pp. 35–52). Mahwah, NJ: Erlbaum.

Berliner, D.C., & Rosenshine, B.V. (1977). The acquisition of knowledge in the classroom. In R.C. Anderson, R.J. Spiro, & W. Montague (Eds.), *Schooling and the acquisition of knowledge* (pp. 375–396). Hillsdale, NJ: Erlbaum.

Bishop, P.A., Reyes, C., & Pflaum, S.W. (2006). Read smarter, not harder: Global reading comprehension strategies. *The Reading Teacher, 60*, 66–69.

Duffy, G.G., & McIntyre, L.D. (1982). A naturalistic study of instructional assistance in primary-grade reading. *The Elementary School Journal, 83*, 15–23.

Evertson, C.M., Emmer, E.T., & Clements, B.S. (1984). *Classroom management for elementary teachers.* Englewood Cliffs, NJ: Prentice Hall.

Frey, N. (2006). How to build great readers. *Teaching Pre K–8, 36*, 1.

Good, T., & Grouws, D. (1979). The Missouri mathematics effectiveness project: An experimental study in fourth-grade classrooms. *Journal of Educational Psychology, 71*, 355–362.

Hill, J.E., & Flynn, K. (2006). *Classroom instruction that works with English language learners.* Alexandria, VA: Association for Supervision and Curriculum Development.

Johnson, R.T., & Johnson, D.W. (1985). Student-student interaction: Ignored but powerful. *Journal of Teacher Education, 36*(4), 22–26.

Kelley, M., & Clausen-Grace, N. (2006). R⁵: The sustained silent reading makeover that transformed readers. *The Reading Teacher, 60*, 148–156.

Kounin, J.S. (1970). *Discipline and group management in classrooms.* New York: Holt, Rinehart and Winston.

Methe, S.A., & Hintze, J.M. (2003). Evaluating teacher modeling as a strategy to increase student reading behavior. *School Psychology Review, 32*, 617–623.

Paris, S.G., Lipson, M.Y., & Wixson, K.K. (1983). Becoming a strategic reader. *Contemporary Educational Psychology, 8*, 293–316.

Singer, H., & Donlan, D. (1989). *Reading and learning from text* (2nd ed.). Hillsdale, NJ: Erlbaum.

Totten, S., Sills, T., Digby, A., & Russ, P. (1991). *Cooperative learning: A guide to research*. New York: Garland.

Vacca, R.T., & Vacca, J.A.L. (2008). *Content area reading: Literacy and learning across the curriculum* (9th ed.). Boston: Allyn & Bacon.

Wood, K.D., & Beattie, J. (2004). Meeting the literacy needs of students with ADHD in the middle school classroom. *Middle School Journal, 35*(3), 50–55.

Wood, K.D., & Tinajero, J. (2002). Using pictures to teach content to second language learners. *Middle School Journal, 33*(5), 47–51.

PART II

Collaborative Guides

Drawing upon sociocultural theory, the guides in this section are designed to foster discussion and require group interaction. Students are preassigned to dyads or small groups and encouraged to share, discuss, and elaborate on each other's responses. The practice of engaging students in discussion of text has ample and long-standing support in the professional literature on literacy.

CHAPTER 3

Collaborative Listening–Viewing Guide

Grade Levels
Primary, intermediate, middle, secondary

Subjects
Science, language arts, social studies, fine arts

Classroom Contexts
Individuals, pairs, small groups

The Collaborative Listening–Viewing Guide (Wood, 1990; Wood, Flood, & Lapp, 1998; Wood & Taylor, 2006) is a framework for taking notes from information observed or heard rather than read. The Collaborative Listening–Viewing Guide concept can be used in many different situations. It can be used as students watch and react to a scientific experiment, listen to a lecture in social studies, observe a streaming video related to a topic in health, or take a cyber tour of a museum in art class. It can also be used as a means to incorporate writing while on a field trip, as is illustrated in Figure 5. Teachers can use this type of guide to help them organize the content they want to present, while students can use it to receive, record, and process the new content with the aid of their peers. One of the main benefits of the Collaborative Listening–Viewing Guide is the reliance on peer interaction—the socially constructed knowledge mentioned in chapter 1 of this text. What one student in the group misses or doesn't understand, another student may remember or clarify. The guide calls for whole-class, small-group, and individualized instruction and learning, a combination that is well-supported in the professional literature on effective teaching (Gambrell, Morrow, & Pressley, 2007).

The Collaborative Listening–Viewing Guide has five phases or components: previewing/reviewing, recording, elaborating, synthesizing, and extending information. First working individually and then working

Figure 5. Second Graders' Reporters Notes on Museum Exhibit of Dinosaurs		
Lauren	Ellie	Kevin
Millions ago	dinosaur lizards	Millions years
terrible lizard	skeletons	T-Rex
Eats Meat	Big teeth	Stands on Back
King	King dinosaurs	King of Dinosaurs
Roars		

From Wood, K.D., Flood, J., & Lapp, D. (1998). Viewing: The neglected communication process or "when what you see isn't what you get." *The Reading Teacher, 52,* 300–304. Reprinted with the permission of the International Reading Association.

in groups of different sizes, students complete a form that has spaces for each component. Below we describe these phases before presenting a sample guide.

Preview/Review

As its name implies, this stage can serve two functions. The preview function operates similarly to the "coming attractions" trailers shown in many movie theaters, which provide the audience with a brief overview of an upcoming film. With the Collaborative Listening–Viewing Guide, the preview may consist of a student-directed activity, a teacher-directed activity, or a combination of the two. A student-directed activity might be a brainstorming session to elicit students' prior knowledge of a particular topic. For example, a teacher may say, "Before we see this video on the Industrial Revolution, let's find out what you already know. I'll organize your responses on the board." An activity that involves more teacher direction and less student input might be the presentation of key concepts and vocabulary that will be encountered in the lesson. A lead-in statement for this activity might be "Our demonstration today will be on static electricity. Because you will hear a few terms that you may not recognize, I'll explain their definitions now and show how each term will be used in the context of the demonstration." The students then write that information in their guides.

The second function of the preview/review phase is to review information already learned from a chapter or unit before introducing a related activity (e.g., a field trip, video, or demonstration). The review reinforces the later activity's goal of solidifying and extending the lesson. The teacher directive in this case might be "We have been studying

Greece. Tell me what you remember about Greek customs, old and new, before we meet our guest from Greece."

Record

In the record phase, students are asked to individually jot down important concepts, phrases, or events as they are listening or viewing. Students should be instructed to keep their notes brief, using abbreviations when possible, so that the transcribing does not interfere with their listening. It is also important that the notes be recorded in sequential order to facilitate the next phase, group elaboration.

In the example shown in Figure 5, second graders were instructed to take notes individually before a field trip to a museum with an exhibition on dinosaurs (Wood, Flood, & Lapp, 1998). Students were heterogeneously grouped in fours ahead of time and were each given an individual reporter's notebook. The teacher modeled how to take notes, draw pictures (an especially useful strategy for English-language learners), and depict in any way they chose what they would see while on the trip.

Elaborate

In this phase, the students join together in previously established small groups to elaborate on their notes from the record phase. Here they can put their heads together to recall details, flesh out their abbreviated notes, contribute related information, and reorganize the material. This phase should take place as soon as possible after the initial listening/viewing lesson to ensure that the students will be able to remember the significant information. For example, Figure 6 illustrates second graders' group

Figure 6. Second Graders' Group Notes on Museum Dinosaur Exhibit		
Lauren	Ellie	Kevin

Dinosaurs means terrible lizard
Lived Millions of years ago
T-rex is king of Dinosaurs
Has Big teeth
Stands on back legs
Eats other Dinosaurs
Roars like a lion

From Wood, K.D., Flood, J., & Lapp, D. (1998). Viewing: The neglected communication process or "when what you see isn't what you get." *The Reading Teacher, 52,* 300–304. Reprinted with the permission of the International Reading Association.

elaboration conducted after their museum field trip. Back in the classroom, each group discussed what they saw and developed a summary paragraph between them that described their findings.

Synthesize

After the groups have met to elaborate on the initially recorded information, the class as a whole should be consulted to provide yet a broader view on the topic and synthesize the groups' collections of information. The teacher may begin this phase by asking, "What are some significant things we have learned from today's observation?" Here is an opportunity to help students make generalizations about the content learned without burdening the discussion with superfluous details. Students can organize and record on their guides the most important concepts contributed by class members.

Extend

The extend phase of the Collaborative Listening–Viewing Guide allows students to work in pairs to apply the information they've learned. For instance, they may compose a paragraph or two consolidating some of the information, design a project related to the topic, develop a semantic map of the key concepts, write a play or skit, or conduct further research on an aspect of interest to them.

Figure 7 provides a sample of a student-completed guide for a video on oceans, excerpted from a lesson in the classroom of Susan Avett, a teacher and literacy coach in Cabarrus County Schools, North Carolina, USA (a reproducible version of this figure can be found on page 176 in the Appendix). The purpose of the video was to provide students with background information and visual reinforcement for a science unit on oceans. In the preview phase the teacher began by eliciting students' preexisting knowledge of the topic in a brainstorming session and introduced a few interesting facts. She also asked students to review the location of the world's oceans by pointing them out on a map. The students then recorded the relevant information individually, as illustrated in the "Preview/Review" section of the figure.

During the video screening, the students recorded key phrases and terms down the left-hand column of the guide, as illustrated in the "Record (individually)" section in the guide. Afterward, the students worked in groups to elaborate on one another's notes, trigger new recollections, and consolidate the information, as shown in the "Elaborate (groups)" section in the right-hand column of the guide. Notice how content missed in the individual note-taking activity was filled in during the elaboration activity as the groups pooled their recalled information.

Figure 7. Collaborative Listening–Viewing Guide for Video on Oceans

Class: Science

Topic: Oceans

Student's name: Kevin

Group members: Lauren, Ryan, Eric

Preview/Review

The world is really one big ocean. 70 percent is water—not as calm as it looks—always moving. Plants and animals (some weigh tons and some can't be seen) can change salt water to fresh water. Ocean bottom is six miles below surface (from our school to fairgrounds). Atlantic, Pacific, Indian, Arctic, Antarctic.

Record (individually)	Elaborate (groups)
World oceans— Pacific is largest	Pacific, Atlantic, and Indian in order of size make up world oceans—also Arctic and Antarctic.
Ocean scientists	Oceanographers are scientists who study the sea.
Swimming easier	Swimming is easier because salt helps us float—contains common table salt.
Blue whales	Ocean is home to the largest animals that ever lived. Blue whales can be 95 ft. Smallest is only 1/25,000 of an inch.
Three types of life Nekton, plankton (jellyfish, small drifting), benthos	Nekton—can swim around like fish, squid, whales, seals. Barracuda can swim at 30 mph. Many fish can't live anywhere in ocean because of temperature and food supply. Plankton—floating, drifting plants and animals (jellyfish). Benthos—plants and animals that live on the bottom of the ocean—sponges, starfish, coral, and oysters—fixed to the bottom and can't move.

Synthesize (whole class)

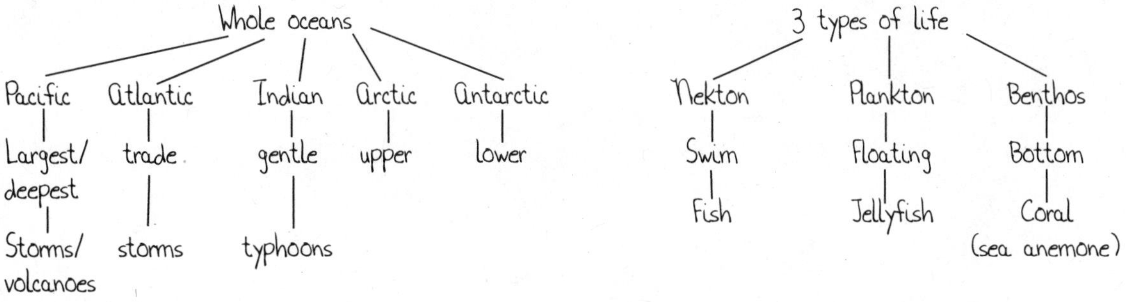

```
              Whole oceans                                    3 types of life
    ┌──────┬──────┴──┬──────┬──────┐              ┌──────────┼──────────┐
 Pacific  Atlantic  Indian  Arctic  Antarctic   Nekton    Plankton    Benthos
    │        │        │       │       │            │          │          │
 Largest/  trade    gentle  upper   lower        Swim      Floating    Bottom
 deepest     │        │                            │          │          │
    │       storms  typhoons                      Fish     Jellyfish    Coral
 Storms/                                                             (sea anemone)
 volcanoes
```

Extend/Apply (pairs)

Our study question for this unit is: How old is the ocean and how did the oceans begin?

Created by literacy specialist Susan Avett. Originally published in Wood, K.D., & Harmon, J.M. (2001). *Strategies for integrating reading and writing in the middle and high school classroom* (p. 91). Westerville, OH: National Middle School Association. Reprinted with the permission of the National Middle School Association.

In the synthesize phase, the entire class was asked to brainstorm and contribute concepts they had learned. With the teacher's help, the students then reorganized this information into semantic maps.

Finally, the students were given a variety of options from which to choose for the extend phase. The partners for this guide chose to come up with a question to research (and eventually answer) using multiple sources during the rest of the unit on oceans.

Tips for Diverse Learners

- Pair an ELL student with another student/tutor to discuss the content of the viewing.
- Use visuals to help reinforce students' learning of English.
- Encourage and model for students how to draw or depict what they see.

REFERENCES

Gambrell, L.B., Morrow, L.M., & Pressley, M. (2007). *Best practices in literacy instruction* (3rd ed.). New York: Guilford.

Wood, K.D. (1990). The collaborative listening-viewing guide: An aid for notetaking. *Middle School Journal, 22*(1), 53–56.

Wood, K.D., Flood, J., & Lapp, D. (1998). Viewing: The neglected communication process or "when what you see isn't what you get." *The Reading Teacher, 52*, 300–304.

Wood, K.D., & Harmon, J.M. (2001). *Strategies for integrating reading and writing in the middle and high school classroom*. Westerville, OH: National Middle School Association.

Wood, K.D., & Taylor, D.B. (2006). *Literacy strategies across the subject areas: Process-oriented blackline masters for the K–12 classroom* (2nd ed.). Boston: Allyn & Bacon.

CHAPTER 4

Interactive Reading Guide

If a major lesson objective is to promote learning through cooperative activities, then the Interactive Reading Guide (described in Buehl, 2001; Wood, 1990, 1992, 2002; Wood & Harmon, 2001) is an appropriate choice. The Interactive Reading Guide is also a good strategy guide to use when you've determined that a group of students—or the whole class—needs additional help with a lesson. This help may include assisting the class in interpreting and recasting information from nontraditional text such as websites, online encyclopedia entries, virtual tours, and the like, which are often written for a broader audience.

Most traditional study guides were designed to be used by students working individually, but with the Interactive Reading Guide, the teacher directs the students' use of the strategy guide and the learning of the content by requiring responses from individuals, pairs, small groups, or the class as a whole. The teacher acts as a conductor, guiding and directing the students, and as a monitor, overseeing the group interactions and providing help when needed. Throughout the lesson, students are asked to make predictions, develop associations, recall what was read (either mentally or in writing), or reorganize information in accordance with the text's structure. In the end, the completed guide will give students a synopsis of the topic content that will be useful for future study and review. Because Interactive Reading Guides require a good deal of oral and graphic response from the students, it may take several days to complete one.

For management purposes, it is helpful to determine the group assignments before beginning the lesson. That way, the students who will

Grade Levels
Primary, intermediate, middle, secondary

Subjects
Reading/language arts, English, math, social studies, science, fine arts

Classroom Contexts
Individuals, small groups, whole class

Guiding Readers Through Text: Strategy Guides for New Times (2nd ed.) by Karen D. Wood, Diane Lapp, James Flood, and D. Bruce Taylor. © 2008 by the International Reading Association.

gain most from peer tutoring can be grouped with others who possess more expertise. After the students complete each segment, activity, or question within the guide, the teacher directs the class in a discussion of the content. The teacher can vary the time spent on each activity as needed. Some segments can be taken slowly, while others may be given a time limit. The more advanced students may be allowed to proceed ahead in certain segments of the guide if the teacher so chooses.

Figure 8 presents a sample Interactive Reading Guide for an intermediate-level lesson on Japan based on a social studies textbook. Students begin by working in groups to write down everything that comes to mind on the topics listed for Japan. Because these topics were taken directly from the chapter's subheadings, the students can readily match their reading to the topics listed on the guide. After the initial free association, the guide leads students through a wide variety of activities designed to engage their interest and improve their understanding. The activities range from whisper reading with a partner to putting two pencils together and pretending to eat with chopsticks. Question 6, which asks students to react to a series of statements before and after reading the section on "Industrialized Japan," is a type of Anticipation Guide (see chapter 11). In the final question, the students are to skim over their responses while keeping in mind the topics introduced at the beginning of the guide. Then, a class discussion follows. This review activity serves to reinforce and synthesize the major concepts just learned.

Figure 9 presents excerpted questions and activities from an Interactive Reading Guide developed for a middle school social studies class on the regions of Eastern Europe. As with the Interactive Reading Guide on Japan featured in Figure 8, students work through the guide in their preassigned groups and pairs. They begin by focusing their attention on the map located in the text. Focusing students' attention on these visual aids is necessary because maps, charts, and graphs are often overlooked by students when reading textbook material. By using the guide, students take turns locating each country to get a sense of the geographic location and become tactilely involved as they trace the Danube River with their fingers. Because the textbook chapter did not contain information about the strife in Kosovo, the teacher, through the guide, was able to lead the class to the Internet where they were asked to seek out current information about the conflicts in the area (see items #4 and #5 in Figure 9). Students are instructed to read online newspaper articles related to the topic and report on their findings to their group members. A lesson such as this one could take place over a week or more and might include activities such as virtual tours of the Balkans, class debates and discussions, streaming video, and teacher lecture. When used with sources such as video or virtual tours or online lecture, the teacher must "pause" the content at an appropriate time to allow the

Chapter 12: Japan—An Island Country

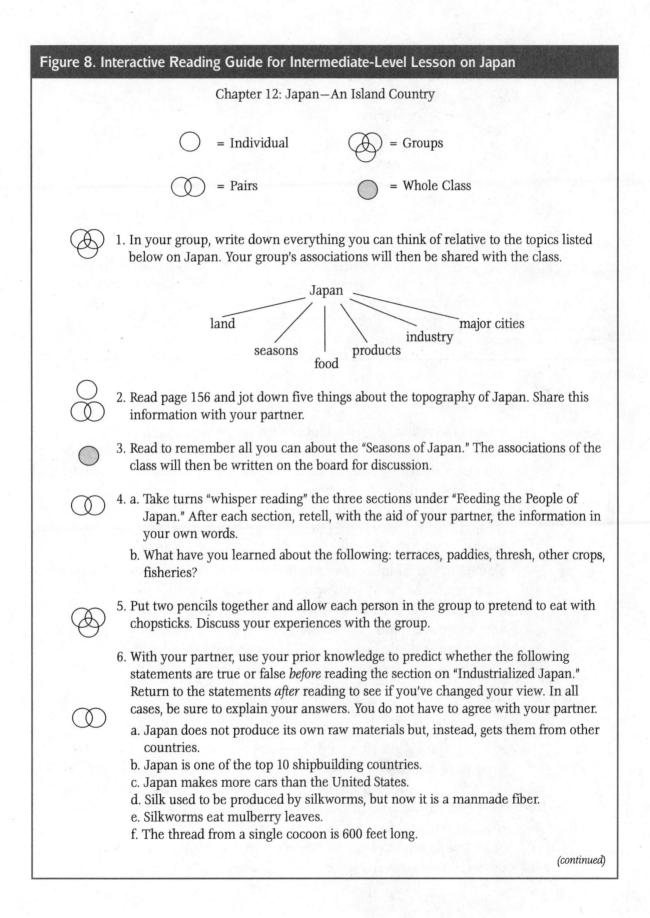

○ = Individual   ⊛ = Groups

⊙ = Pairs   ● = Whole Class

1. In your group, write down everything you can think of relative to the topics listed below on Japan. Your group's associations will then be shared with the class.

Japan

land   seasons   food   products   industry   major cities

2. Read page 156 and jot down five things about the topography of Japan. Share this information with your partner.

3. Read to remember all you can about the "Seasons of Japan." The associations of the class will then be written on the board for discussion.

4. a. Take turns "whisper reading" the three sections under "Feeding the People of Japan." After each section, retell, with the aid of your partner, the information in your own words.

   b. What have you learned about the following: terraces, paddies, thresh, other crops, fisheries?

5. Put two pencils together and allow each person in the group to pretend to eat with chopsticks. Discuss your experiences with the group.

6. With your partner, use your prior knowledge to predict whether the following statements are true or false *before* reading the section on "Industrialized Japan." Return to the statements *after* reading to see if you've changed your view. In all cases, be sure to explain your answers. You do not have to agree with your partner.

   a. Japan does not produce its own raw materials but, instead, gets them from other countries.

   b. Japan is one of the top 10 shipbuilding countries.

   c. Japan makes more cars than the United States.

   d. Silk used to be produced by silkworms, but now it is a manmade fiber.

   e. Silkworms eat mulberry leaves.

   f. The thread from a single cocoon is 600 feet long.

(continued)

7. After reading, write down three new things you learned about the following topics:
    Other industries of Japan
    Old and new ways of living

Compare these responses with those of your group.

8. Read the section on "Cities of Japan." Each group member is to choose a city, show its location on the map, and find additional information on the Internet to share with your group.

9. Return to the major topics introduced in the first activity. Skim over your chapter reading guide responses with these topics in mind. Next, be ready to contribute, along with the class, anything you have learned about these topics.

From Wood, K.D. (1988). Guiding students through informational text. *The Reading Teacher, 41,* 912–920. Reprinted with the permission of the International Reading Association

students to reflect, discuss, and engage in the designated activity. At the conclusion of the lesson, the students are asked to return to the guide, skim over their responses, and be ready to contribute their newly learned knowledge with class members.

When applied to mathematics, the Interactive Reading Guide helps students see the processes involved in solving word and computation problems (Wood, 1990). The guide shown in Figure 10 is for an elementary-level lesson on two-digit divisors. For illustration purposes, we've made the guide somewhat more verbose than it would normally be. In class, the teacher would include the needed explanation in a verbal demonstration rather than presenting the extensive information shown in the guide in Figure 10. This teacher explanation and scaffolding would eventually lead to the abbreviated form in Figure 11. In order to begin the scaffolding process, the teacher should thoroughly model the guide, "walking" students through it step by step. The teacher could model the "talking aloud" portion, initially mentioned in item number 1 of Figure 10, by thinking out loud and writing down each procedure one step at a time; for example, the teacher could say, "Let's see, first I would see if 22 goes into 11.... Second...." After the students have had sufficient experience with an Interactive Reading Guide on math topics, for example, all a teacher would need to do is put the grouping codes and page numbers on the board in abbreviated form as depicted in Figure 11.

◯	= Individual
◯◯	= Pairs
◯◯◯	= Groups
●	= Whole Class

1. Look at the map on page 347.
   a. Take turns locating each country (see chart at bottom of page) on the map. What are these nations called?
   b. Name and locate three mountain regions.
   c. Locate the Danube River. Trace it with your finger.

2. a. Mumble read the introduction on page 348 and talk to your partner about **when** and **why** the ancestors of the Hungarians moved South.
   b. With your partner, locate the word *diversity*. Write down the three different ways it is used on page 348. Talk over the ways societies can benefit from diversity.

3. Whisper read the first two paragraphs (page 350) with your partner to find out why ethnic differences remain for (a) the Jewish people and (b) the Gypsies.

4. Use the Internet to find a map and information about Kosovo and describe (a) its location and (b) its leader.

5. What is the cause of the conflict in this area? How is it similar to or different from other conflicts in this area about which you have read? What is missing from the textbook's discussion of this topic?

6. Read the online newspaper article about "ethnic cleansing" and discuss with your group members the implications of this practice for the region and the world. What is the author trying to get you to believe?

From Wood, K.D. (2002). Tutors in print form: Using study guides to develop multiple literacies. *Middle Ground*, 6(2),10–14. Reprinted with the permission of the National Middle School Association.

○	= Individual
◯◯	= Pairs
◯◯◯	= Groups
⬤	= Whole Class

1. In your groups, work through the sample problem at the top of page 108. Designate one person as the "thinker" to talk through the thinking processes involved and one person as the "writer" to write down the steps. The other members of the group should contribute their thinking, too.

   Hint: The writer can use chart paper so that all group members can see the steps.

2. Work through the first two problems in the "Study and Learn" section. Repeat the same procedures as in Question 1, but this time assign different group members the roles of thinker and writer.

3. In pairs, work through the next two problems in the "Study and Learn" section, "talking aloud" the process with your partner. Then compare your computations with those of the others in your group. If there is disagreement anywhere in your computations, talk through the processes used.

4. In pairs, work through problems 5 to 12 in the "Divide and Check" section. Compare your computations with those of the rest of your group and discuss any disagreements.

5. Work through the next 10 problems individually. Check and discuss any disagreements with your partner.

6. Talk yourself through and write out the steps for the two word problems in the "Solve Problems" section. Compare answers with the rest of your group and discuss your thinking.

7. With your partner, make up two more word problems that involve dividing by two digits. Work through the answers. Exchange word problems with your group and compare processes.

From Wood, K.D., Lapp, D., & Flood, J. (1992). *Guiding readers through text: A review of study guides* (p. 21). Newark, DE: International Reading Association.

Figure 11. Abbreviated Interactive Reading Guide for Math Lesson

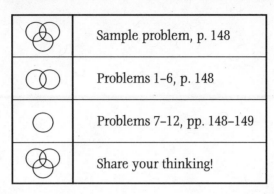

⊕	Sample problem, p. 148
⊘	Problems 1–6, p. 148
○	Problems 7–12, pp. 148–149
⊕	Share your thinking!

From Wood, K.D. (1992). Fostering collaborative reading and writing. *Journal of Reading, 36*, 96–103. Reprinted with the permission of the International Reading Association.

Tips for Diverse Learners

- Group students to ensure that the ELL student has an English-speaking buddy as a partner.
- Provide thorough monitoring of paired and group work.
- When creating an Interactive Reading Guide for your classroom, provide activities that relate to pictures in the text or visuals from printed or online sources that relate to the topic under study.

REFERENCES

Buehl, D. (2001). *Classroom strategies for interactive learning* (2nd ed.). Newark, DE: International Reading Association.

Wood, K.D. (1988). Guiding students through informational text. *The Reading Teacher, 41*, 912–920.

Wood, K.D. (1990, June). *Collaborative strategies for improving students' conceptual understanding of mathematics.* Paper presented at the MacMillan Symposium on Mathematics and Science, Santa Fe, NM.

Wood, K.D. (1992). Fostering collaborative reading and writing experiences in mathematics. *Journal of Reading, 36*, 96–103.

Wood, K.D. (2002). Tutors in print form: Using study guides to develop multiple literacies. *Middle Ground, 6*(2), 10–14.

Wood, K.D., & Harmon, J.M. (2001). *Strategies for integrating reading and writing in middle and high school classrooms.* Westerville, OH: National Middle School Association.

Wood, K.D., Lapp, D., & Flood, J. (1992). *Guiding readers through text: A review of study guides.* Newark, DE: International Reading Association.

CHAPTER 5

Reciprocal Teaching Discussion Guide

Reciprocal Teaching, developed by Palincsar and Brown (1984), is a well-known instructional technique for supporting students' application of comprehension strategies as they engage in classroom dialogues. This versatile teaching tool has an extensive research base supporting its effectiveness across age groups from grade 4 through adult, across differing ability levels, and even across various subject matter areas (Klingner & Vaughn, 1996). The Reciprocal Teaching Discussion Guide can help teachers support student engagement with Reciprocal Teaching.

Reciprocal Teaching has several important features (Palincsar & Brown, 1984). First, Reciprocal Teaching is used with authentic classroom texts, and its design promotes instructional conversations between teacher and students. Reciprocal teaching also focuses on the gradual release of responsibility as students eventually take over the conversations without the teacher. Most importantly, it highlights four critical comprehension strategies: predicting, questioning, clarifying, and summarizing. Predicting is a universal, fundamental strategy for comprehending; it involves thinking ahead, anticipating what might happen, and making an informed guess. The questioning strategy guides readers' thinking as they wonder about ideas presented in the text or try to decipher what the author is trying to say. Formulating questions then leads readers in the search for clarification. Clarifying can occur individually when a student self-monitors and takes action to find the answer to an unfamiliar word or to reconsider what the author is saying. Clarifying also occurs in group settings where one student can offer

Grade Levels
Intermediate, middle, secondary

Subjects
Reading/language arts, social studies, science, fine arts

Classroom Contexts
Individuals, small groups, whole class, tutoring sessions

Guiding Readers Through Text: Strategy Guides for New Times (2nd ed.) by Karen D. Wood, Diane Lapp, James Flood, and D. Bruce Taylor. © 2008 by the International Reading Association.

explanations to another. Summarizing involves determining important ideas and then retelling these ideas in a new way.

The Reciprocal Teaching Discussion Guide provides a concrete structure to help teachers model the strategy and to help students begin the Reciprocal Teaching conversations. However, it is not designed to be used as an end product but rather as a way to help students gather their thoughts about their reading and to guide their use of these four comprehension strategies. The guide is flexible enough to be used with individual students in tutoring situations, with small-group instruction, and with whole classes. Reciprocal Teaching itself works with both narrative and informational texts.

Students begin by making predictions about the passage they will be reading. As they read, they will either confirm or disconfirm their predictions and provide evidence to support their thoughts. Once reading continues, the students then generate questions they may have about what they are reading. These questions may be ideas they are wondering about or may be questions about some confusing section of the text. In this part of the guide, students write their questions in the second and third columns. Once the questions are written, students then engage in a group discussion where they present their questions and seek clarification from others. These ideas are then written in the appropriate section of the guide. Working with the group, students can review their guide and then generate two or three important ideas to include in a summary of the text. While the four strategies in the guide are presented in a particular order, students do not necessarily need to follow this order. Sometimes questions may arise first before predictions.

The Reciprocal Teaching Discussion Guide in Figure 12 illustrates how Reciprocal Teaching may work during a tutoring session with a struggling adolescent reader (see page 177 in the Appendix for a reproducible version of the Reciprocal Teaching Discussion Guide). The guide can help a tutee to keep a record of his predictions throughout the reading, and it can also help him understand the value of predictions through confirming and disconfirming his ideas. The tutee can think more deeply about the predictions by finding supporting evidence in the text. The questions written in the guide by the tutee can serve as the basis for discussion where both the tutee and tutor clarify ideas and finally summarize the important ideas of the text passage.

The example in Figure 13 demonstrates the use of the Reciprocal Teaching Discussion Guide with secondary students as they read, discuss, and write about the topic of school uniforms. Both examples reaffirm the versatility of the Reciprocal Teaching process to help all students actively engage in literacy activities.

Figure 12. Intermediate- or Secondary-Level Reciprocal Teaching Discussion Guide for Article on Teens and Respect

Text Examined

Coleman, Ashlee. (2006, October). "Teens Deserve Respect, Too." *North New Jersey Media Group.* Retrieved October 11, 2006, from www.northjersey.com

Synopsis of Article

A high school junior writes about the seeming unfairness with which adults treat teens. She recounts instances of teachers using sarcasm to humiliate her fellow students and parents whose "let's be friends" parenting approach backfires when their children open up about their lives. All she asks is that adults "be real" and stop being hypocritical in their treatment of teens.

Predict

Make a prediction about each passage after you read the title.	Confirm or disconfirm your prediction.	Provide evidence from the book to support your thoughts.
1. Parents should respect teens. 2. Teens don't get respect. 3. Adults think teens will do something bad. 4. Something bad happened to her (the author). 5. She wants respect.	1. Yes 2. Yes 3. No 4. Yes 5. Yes	• The whole article • 4th paragraph "invading our space" • Her teacher was sarcastic to her

Read

Question What wonderings do you have about this passage? Is there something that is confusing to you? Write one or two questions that you have about this passage.	Question Why can the teachers be sarcastic but the students can't?	Question Why do teachers read notes aloud?
Discuss Pose your questions to the group.	⇩	⇩
Clarify Write any clarifications made by the group members.	• The students should be able to be sarcastic if the teacher is. • The teachers can write you up.	• Teachers reading notes aloud is an example of invading the students' personal space.

(continued)

Figure 12. Intermediate- or Secondary-Level Reciprocal Teaching Discussion Guide for Article on Teens and Respect (continued)

Summarize

Write two or three ideas you think are important to remember about this passage. Share these points with your group.

1. Teachers should read this article.
2. Adults don't have respect for teens, but they should.
3. The purpose of this article is to help students get respect from adults.

Then, as a group, decide which of the ideas are the most important to include in a group summary of the passage. Write the summary below in three or four sentences.

Adults don't have respect for teens. This article is trying to help teens get respect from adults. Teachers should read this article so they can give teens respect without being nosy.

Created by preservice teacher Valerie Molbert of the University of Texas at San Antonio, USA. Reprinted with permission.

Figure 13. Secondary-Level Reciprocal Teaching Discussion Guide for Article on School Uniforms

Text Examined

Benson, Jessica. (2006, December). "School Officials to Push for High School Uniforms." *The Eagle-Tribune*. Retrieved December 1, 2006, from www.eagletribune.com

Synopsis of Article

A school board is pushing for the institution of uniforms for high school students. The school board had abandoned this idea eight years prior because of student and parent protests. A uniform policy has been in place for elementary and middle schools in the area. However, because of school violence and a new high school being built, the issue of school uniforms for high school students has been raised again, this time by the parents. Because a majority of the parents and the board members are in favor of uniforms, the proposal has a good chance of passing this time.

Predict

Make a prediction about this passage after you read the title.	Confirm or disconfirm your prediction.	Provide evidence from the book to support your thoughts.
1. The school board wants students to wear uniforms. 2. The parents might not want the uniforms, considering the fact that the school has to push for them. 3. The students might not want uniforms, for the same reason.	1. Yes 2. No 3. No	• "high school officials think the time has come to require the city's h.s. students to wear uniforms" • "the proposal has a chance to be approved bc it was brought forward by the parents" • "the practice will not be that different from what many students and their parents in Lawrence are already accustomed [to]"

(continued)

Read

Question What wonderings do you have about this passage? Is there something that is confusing to you? Write one or two questions that you have about this passage.	Question • Why didn't the proposal go through eight years ago? • Why are the parents wanting uniforms now, all of a sudden? • Is it true that Latino parents are used to uniforms?	Question • Why do they need a subcommittee if everyone wants the uniforms? • Why did the parents and students protest uniforms back when it was first required? • What makes the uniforms "fit in well with a new school building"?
Discuss Pose your questions to the group.	⬇	⬇
Clarify Write any clarifications made by the group members.	• Maybe the parents didn't think uniforms were necessary, or they didn't like them. • The article says school safety and a new school are being used as arguments for the uniforms. • I don't know if it's true. Maybe Latino countries have more Catholic schools, and Catholic schools have uniforms.	• It's part of their rules. They have to have a subcommittee as part of the process. • Maybe they thought the students weren't as violent as they are today. Maybe the parents thought the cost of uniforms was too much. • Maybe the new building is a new start and the uniforms will look nice. School colors or something.

Summarize

Write two or three ideas you think are important to remember about this passage. Share these points with your group.

1. The parents and school board want to make students wear uniforms for safety reasons.

2. Now that the parents want uniforms, the proposal will pass this time.

3. The elementary and middle school students already have to wear uniforms.

Then, as a group, decide which of the ideas are the most important to include in a group summary of the passage. Write the summary below in three or four sentences.

The school board at Lawrence is trying to pass a proposal to make students wear uniforms. The proposal didn't pass eight years ago because the parents and students protested. Now the parents want the uniforms, so the proposal might pass this time. Their reasons are school safety and the uniforms will look good with the new building. They had to form a subcommittee to study the proposal. But because the parents and the school board members want the uniforms, it will probably pass.

Created by preservice teacher Valerie Molbert of the University of Texas at San Antonio, USA. Reprinted with permission.

Tips for Diverse Learners

- Have ELLs work with a small group of learners whose first language is English.
- Encourage ELLs to highlight unfamiliar vocabulary for questioning.
- Have other students clarify vocabulary for ELLs.
- Encourage the use of newly learned vocabulary in the summarizing section if feasible.

REFERENCES

Klingner, J.K., & Vaughn, S. (1996). Reciprocal teaching of reading comprehension strategies for students with learning disabilities who use English as a second language. *The Elementary School Journal, 96,* 275–293.

Palincsar, A.S., & Brown, A.L. (1984). Reciprocal teaching of comprehension-fostering and comprehension-monitoring activities. *Cognition and Instruction, 1,* 117–175.

PART III

Thinking Guides

The need to engage students in higher order thinking processes has a long history in the professional literature in reading. While all of the guides in this book encourage students to read beyond the literal level, the guides in this section are specifically designed to encourage deeper processing of informational and narrative traditional and nontraditional text. Consequently, we have termed the guides *thinking guides* because their primary purpose is to help students critically analyze, interpret, question, and synthesize information from varied sources.

Critical Profiler Guide

Today's students interact with a diverse array of information sources, and as they read they frequently transact with text from an emotional or factual stance (McLaughlin & DeVoogd, 2004; Rosenblatt, 2002). While it is essential that readers gather information from the author as well as interpret the author's meaning, we want to help readers move forward in their comprehension development so they can become thoughtful consumers of texts. The basic rationale to consider, then, is that we don't want our readers to assume that because it is stated in a text, it must be true. Therefore, it is important for today's teachers to teach their students to read with a critical eye. Reading from a critical stance requires both the ability and the deliberate tendency to think critically about texts, to analyze and evaluate information sources (such as traditional print texts, multimedia sources, music lyrics, and hypertexts), to meaningfully question their origin and purpose, and to take action by presenting alternative perspectives.

Therefore, the Critical Profiler Guide, designed and implemented by doctoral student and middle school teacher Lina Soares, addresses the critical stance, requiring readers to tap into their prior knowledge to comprehend the relationship between their thoughts and the views presented from the author's perspective. The purpose of the Critical Profiler Guide is to guide students through a learning process that teaches them to question as they read or interact with a text, to know the author's intent, to understand the sociocultural influences on the text, and to comprehend with a critical edge. Because this is a new approach for some students, students can choose to work in pairs or small groups, and the strategy can be modified to accommodate ELL needs.

Text selections chosen for this lesson should provide a scaffolded reading experience (Graves & Graves, 1994). Prior to completing the

Grade Levels
Intermediate, middle, secondary

Subjects
Reading/language arts, social studies, science, fine arts

Classroom Contexts
Individuals, small groups, whole class, tutoring sessions

Guiding Readers Through Text: Strategy Guides for New Times (2nd ed.) by Karen D. Wood, Diane Lapp, James Flood, and D. Bruce Taylor. © 2008 by the International Reading Association.

Critical Profiler Guide, prereading activities should prepare students for the reading selections by preteaching aspects of the reading lesson and tapping into prior knowledge. Likewise, during-reading activities should include questions to stimulate students' inquiry and to allow students to obtain specific information and understand the overall message. The combination of prereading, during-reading, and the Critical Profiler Guide activities provides opportunities for students to organize and synthesize information from the text so that they can evaluate the authors' points, his or her stance in presenting the messages, and provide further opportunities for students to respond to text in a variety of ways.

For example, in an upper elementary–level classroom, the Critical Profiler Guide can be used in a language arts/social studies lesson on *The Trail on Which They Wept: The Story of a Cherokee Girl* (Hoobler & Hoobler, 1992), a narrative based on the federal removal and forced relocation policy for Native Americans. By using the Critical Profiler Guide with this book, students will be able to recognize examples of prejudice and to identify cultural factors that influenced events. Students should be given the time and opportunity to understand that texts are authored from a particular perspective and that becoming critically aware involves questioning the text and engaging in actions that represent alternative views. In addition, while the lesson models steps that can be taken to guide students to think from a critical stance, it also demonstrates how to integrate the text and information obtained from Internet resources.

Before introducing the guide, you can provide the foundation for students to read this text from a critical stance by using prereading activities such as the following:

- Before beginning *The Trail on Which They Wept*, tell students they will learn about the effects of western expansion and how the relationship between the Native Americans and the white settlers began to change. Have students create a timeline from 1820 to 1907, highlighting the main events of western expansion.
- Discuss the Indian Removal Act of 1830 and have students research a map of the Trail of Tears to understand the magnitude of the Cherokee relocation.
- Ask students to read accounts of Cherokee quotes and analyze the impact of the Indian Removal Act of 1830 from different perspectives (see Mintz, 2007).

Then, to help students analyze perspectives and build critical awareness during reading, tell students you are going to model for them how to think critically by analyzing and evaluating the textual material and by deliberately questioning the author's perspective. The following are questions that can be used to scaffold the reading of this book from a critical stance:

- What does the author feel about the relationship between the Cherokee and the white settlers?
- Does the author address how the Cherokee and white Americans could peacefully exist? How?
- How does the author explain Andrew Jackson's removal policy?
- How does the author explain John Marshall's Supreme Court decision?
- Is the Supreme Court's decision realistic and if so why or why not?
- How can a president and states disregard a Supreme Court decision?
- Was Jackson's policy just or unjust?
- What might have been a better policy for the Cherokee?

The key is to encourage speculation and guide any student concern about the topic. Accordingly, while demonstrating this critical strategy, encourage students to respond to the open-ended questions so that they may become familiar with thinking from a critical stance. A possible exchange between the teacher and students during reading might play like this:

Teacher: I am wondering how the authors feel about the relationship between the white settlers and the Cherokee. How would you describe the authors' feelings about the white Americans and the Native Americans?

Student 1: Well, the author doesn't give us too many clues. It's almost like the author does not take a stand one way or the other.

Student 2: Yeah, well, that's a good thing, right?

Student 3: In a way, but that's not what I think. I think the author tells us that the white Americans needed the land and the land was for the taking.

Teacher: That is a good point because during the reading I continued to ask myself why is it not mentioned that there was enough land to share? This leads me to ask whether the authors address how white Americans and Cherokee could peacefully coexist.

When students have finished reading and viewing the full selections, it is a good idea to reinforce and extend learning by having the students respond to questions that promote reading from a critical stance

(McLaughlin & DeVoogd, 2004) and complete one or more of the related activities listed in the Critical Profiler Guide in Figure 14 (see page 178 in the Appendix for a reproducible version of the Critical Profiler Guide). These strategies engage students to review what they have learned and state in their own words from a critical stance.

Similarly, secondary-level students can also gain background knowledge about influences that underlie the issues of prejudice by using a Critical Profiler Guide to view the courtroom scenes in the film *To Kill a Mockingbird* (Mulligan, 1962). Students engage in various activities designed to give them opportunities to use language persuasively in addressing a particular issue, to select an issue and take a stance, and to use argumentation to interpret researched information effectively. The lesson also enhances students' skills in critical media literacy by requiring students to research information on the Internet prior to watching the film.

When using this strategy, teachers can provide the foundation for students to read from a critical stance by using prereading activities such as the following:

- Ask students to share their word knowledge about the terms *prosecution*, *defense*, *testimony*, *summation*, and *verdict*.

- Lead a discussion about the court system of the United States and have students research Supreme Court decisions involving civil rights and discrimination (see Social Studies Help Center, 2006).

- Follow with a discussion on recent controversial court cases involving civil rights.

It is imperative to explain to students that by thinking and questioning out loud, you are positioning yourself to envision an alternate view of the material and you are moving into the role of a text critic. To keep students curious about the function of the text, possible questions to model for *To Kill a Mockingbird* during the viewing of the film are as follows:

- Who was called for the prosecution in *To Kill a Mockingbird*? What testimony did each present?

- Who was called for the defense? What testimony did each present?

- What does the videographer want you to notice about the prosecutor?

- What does the videographer want you to notice about the defense?

- What evidence was presented that alluded to the defendant's guilt? Innocence?

- Could you analyze and evaluate the prosecutor's and the defense's closing arguments to the jury?

Figure 14. Critical Profiler Guide for Elementary-Level Students on *The Trail on Which They Wept*

Critical Profiler Guide
The Trail on Which They Wept

After-Reading, Critical Stance Questions	Student Response After Reading	Student Follow-Up Alternative View (Choose One)
• Whose viewpoint is expressed? • What do the authors want us to believe? • Whose voices are silent, missing, or discounted? • How might alternative perspectives be represented? • How would that contribute to your understanding the text from a critical stance? • What action might you take on the basis of what you have learned? • Do the authors provoke empathy for the Indians?	The white settlers have the loudest voices. They have the power of the president speaking for them and the army to back their voices up. It seems the authors want us to believe that the Indians had no rights to their land. President Jackson's voice was heard the loudest. John Ross spoke for the Cherokees, but his voice wasn't heard. Not even all the Cherokees listened. The authors make it sound like John Ross gave in, but he fought against the Treaty Party. He went to war against his own people who gave in to the government. The authors do make me feel sorry for the Cherokee, but there are too many questions not answered. Is there still a treaty? What does the government do today for the Cherokee?	• Write a speech that you would deliver to President Jackson. Take a stand on the Indian Removal Act of 1830. • Write an editorial for a newspaper expressing your views on westward expansion and its impact on Native Americans in 1830. • Make a visual illustration that demonstrates the Cherokee losses: natural resources, religion, reservation life, culture, and disease. • Create a slide presentation that describes the changing relationships between white Americans and Indians. Present your images to the class. • Have the class pretend they are members of the Cherokee National Council. Ask them to prepare a debate, based on historical evidence, then ask them to vote on whether they should or should not approve the Treaty of New Echota.

Created by doctoral student Lina Soares of the University of North Carolina at Charlotte, USA. Reprinted with permission.

- Does the videographer illustrate the dynamics of prejudice at work in the courtroom?
- How is the jury affected by the sociocultural influences shown in the video?

As with the previous student–teacher interaction example from *The Trail on Which They Wept*, the role of the teacher during the viewing is to model reading from a critical stance in everyday teaching and learning activities. An exchange between the teacher and students in a discussion about the film *To Kill a Mockingbird* might sound like this:

Teacher: You know, I am thinking about an important quote from the text that seems applicable in the courtroom. I quote, "One or two of the jury looked like dressed-up Cunninghams." Is this quote making reference to the issue of prejudice, and how does the videographer illustrate the dynamics of prejudice at work in the courtroom?

Student 1: I think the quote refers to the fact that the jury reflects a mob mentality.

Student 2: Oh yeah, I agree. The videographer reflects the prejudice in the courtroom by showing that justice is separate, kinda like the lives of the jury show the racial and the social stratification that exists in the town.

Teacher: So you are saying that the courtroom is an accurate mirror of the town of Maycomb's people?

Student 2: Definitely, I can see from the film that the members of the jury have a particular mind-set for or against something, and they are against Tom Robinson.

Teacher: What does this say about the sociocultural influences at work in the courtroom?

Student 3: The mob mentality of the town allowed the residents to believe that Tom Robinson was guilty, and this racial prejudice has contaminated the jury.

As in the elementary-level example, when students have finished viewing the full selections, it is a good idea to reinforce and extend learning by having the students respond to questions that promote reading from a critical stance by completing one or more of the related activities planned in the Critical Profiler Guide for *To Kill a Mockingbird* found in Figure 15.

Figure 15. Critical Profiler Guide for Secondary-Level Students on *To Kill A Mockingbird*

Critical Profiler Guide
To Kill a Mockingbird

After-Viewing, Critical Stance Questions	Student Response After Viewing	Student Follow-Up Alternative View (Choose One)
• Who is in the video courtroom scene? • Why are they there? • What does the videographer want you to think? • Who or what is missing from the video? • Who is silenced or discounted? • What might an alternative video show? • How would that contribute to your understanding the video from a critical stance? • What action might you take on the basis of what you have viewed?	It is clear that Tom Robinson is the "mockingbird" in the courtroom, and his only mistake was pity. He is silenced by the racial bigotry, and truth is silenced and discounted. The voice that is heard the most is Mayella's when she says, "I got something to say and then I ain't gonna say no more." She is asserting the social correctness of her (white) story over anything that Tom might say. The jury in the end believes her because they all have to live with each other. An alternative video might show Atticus winning the trial. He is already perceived to be the one member in that society that poses a different value and he is portrayed as one who goes against the norm. Because his values for human dignity can be seen in the video, it would be believable to have him convince the jury and have them give a not guilty verdict.	• Assume the role of a reporter covering the trial. Write about your personal experiences while watching the events of the trial unfold. Take a stance and defend or amend the trial. • Assume the role of Tom Robinson. Write your journal entry the night before the verdict is given. What are your concerns? Fears? Hopes? • Assume the role of Atticus Finch. Write your journal entry the night before your closing argument. What are your concerns? Fears? Hopes? • Assume the role of a jury member. Write your views on the trial and how you reached your decision. Do you defend your position, or if you had a second chance what position would you reach?

Created by doctoral student Lina Soares of the University of North Carolina at Charlotte, USA. Reprinted with permission.

Tips for Diverse Learners

- Pair an ELL student with an English-proficient student.
- Provide a list of the critical vocabulary prior to reading a novel and/or viewing a film.
- Provide ELL students with a bilingual dictionary in English and their native language.
- Plan assessment modification.

REFERENCES

Graves, M.F., & Graves, B.B. (1994). *Scaffolding reading experiences*. Norwood, MA: Christopher-Gordon.

McLaughlin, M., & DeVoogd, G. (2004). Critical literacy as comprehension: Expanding reader response. *Journal of Adolescent & Adult Literacy*, *48*, 52–62.

Mintz, S. (2007). Native American Voices. *Digital History* [Online textbook]. Retrieved January 3, 2007, from www.digitalhistory.uh.edu/native_voices/native_voices.cfm

Rosenblatt, L.M. (2002). The transactional theory of reading and writing. In R.B. Ruddell & N.J. Unrau (Eds.), *Theoretical models and processes of reading* (5th ed., pp. 1363–1398). Newark, DE: International Reading Association.

Social Studies Help Center. (2006). *The Supreme Court*. Retrieved January 6, 2007, from www.socialstudieshelp.com/The_Supreme_Court.htm.

FILM AND LITERATURE CITED

Hoobler, D., & Hoobler, T. (1992). *The trail on which they wept: The story of a Cherokee girl*. Morristown, NJ: Silver Burdett.

Mulligan, R. (Director). (1962). *To kill a mockingbird* [Motion picture]. United States: Universal.

CHAPTER 7

Inquiry Guide

Inquiry Guides (or I-Guides) are an adaptation of the I-chart (Hoffman, 1992), which is featured in several content area literacy texts and is used to guide formal and informal research and inquiry-based learning. I-Guides help students organize and synthesize what they already know with what they learn about a topic as they read about that topic using multiple sources. I-Guides can be used from the intermediate through high school grades (3–12) and, as with I-charts, work well across subject areas.

The creation of I-Guides can be broken into the following steps.

Step 1: Topic. In many cases, the teacher selects the primary topic of study. The teacher may also identify subtopics or themes, but these can be generated by students in a brainstorming session. Broad topics such as World War II, for instance, can be broken into smaller primary topics like the Pacific, European, and North African campaigns with subtopics for each.

Step 2: Prior Knowledge and Reading Plan. Individually or in groups, students write down what they already know about the topic and subtopics, and then with the help of the teacher, identify texts—whether they be textbooks, trade books, videos, websites, software, or other text types—that help them gather information about the subtopics or themes.

Step 3: Reading/Research. Students document key information, addressing major subtopics or themes and using multiple sources. Students list these different sources in the first column of the I-Guide and, where appropriate, fill in information they learn from each source about each subtopic or theme.

Step 4: Summary. Finally, students summarize what they have learned from each text and about each subtopic or theme. This information can

Grade Levels
Intermediate, middle, secondary

Subjects
Reading/language arts, social studies, science, fine arts

Classroom Contexts
Individuals, small groups

Guiding Readers Through Text: Strategy Guides for New Times (2nd ed.) by Karen D. Wood, Diane Lapp, James Flood, and D. Bruce Taylor. © 2008 by the International Reading Association.

then be used to produce a formal or informal report, conduct further inquiry, or share with others in presentations. I-Guides are also valuable study tools.

This process is illustrated in Figures 16 and 17, completed by fourth-grade students and their teacher, who collaborated on an inquiry project in a science unit exploring different power systems. The class brainstormed ideas, and this group decided to learn more about how internal combustion engines work in cars. With the help of their teacher, the group identified three subtopics: combustion, the electrical system, and the cooling system. After writing down what they knew in pencil on an I-chart (see Figure 16), they went to the school library and found two books and a website that helped them learn more about this topic. They fleshed out their ideas and synthesized the information on an I-Guide using a computer to type in the information (see Figure 17; see page 179 in the Appendix for a reproducible version of the guide). With the help of their teacher and a classroom assistant, the students developed a PowerPoint presentation that they shared with students in their class.

I-Guides can help students in several ways. We believe that I-Guides can increase student motivation and engagement because they allow students to negotiate with teachers on topics of inquiry. While teachers and curriculum may dictate the larger topic of learning, students can work to identify individual areas of inquiry within that unit. In addition, I-Guides help foster comprehension by tapping into students' prior knowledge on a topic. Comprehension may also be enhanced as students collaborate and discuss what they know about a topic and what they are learning. The social and discursive nature of learning are vital to mastering new information and concepts (Vygotsky, 1962/1986). I-Guides also encourage multiple-source research without overwhelming students as some traditional methods of information gathering—such as note cards and outlines—may do. Finally, I-Guides encourage students to evaluate information and make judgments about the relative importance of individual sources.

Tips for Diverse Learners

- In order not to overwhelm ELL students, preteach key vocabulary and concepts.
- Pair ELL students with other students—if possible with multilingual students who have competency in English and the students' primary language.
- Limit the scope of inquiry so that ELL students can focus on learning a manageable amount of content. Stress depth over breadth of knowledge.

My Topic How cars work

I-Chart

My Questions	How do engines work?			How will cars work in the future
What I Know	engine makes cars go	Batteries need to be changed		
Book How Things Work Today (Wright & Patel)	Most engines are in the front of the car Engines use oil (why?) What happens when oil gets old?	The fan cools the engine The oil makes the engine parts slippery or smooth	lubricate—to make smooth or slippery	
Book 20th Century Inventions Cars (Oxlade)	A generator makes electricity when the car is running. When you turn off the car you turn off electricity.	The battery gives power to start the car. Then the generator gives the power.		
Book _____				

Diagram

Generator makes electricity → Runs the car → Charges the battery → The battery starts the engine

Figure 17. Fourth-Grade Students' Final Inquiry Guide on How Cars Work

	Major Subtopics or Themes				
Primary Topic: How combustion engines work in cars	Combustion	Electrical system	Cooling system and lubrication	Summary or synthesis of each text	Importance of information
What We Know	Cars can't go without gas.	The battery needs to be charged.	Engines get hot.	Engines have parts like the battery and gas that make them work.	
Source 1: How Things Work Today (Wright & Patel, 2000)	Most engines are in the front of the car. Most engines have 4, 6, or 8 cylinders.	The battery gives power to start the car.	Engines use oil. The oil makes the engine parts slippery or smooth.	The electrical parts help start the car, and oil keeps the engine running smoothly.	1 2 3 ④ 5 Not Helpful Very Helpful
Source 2: 20th Century Inventions (Oxlade, 1997)		A generator makes electricity when the car is running and charges the battery.	The radiator is another part that helps keep the engine cool.	There are many parts to each system in a car.	1 2 ③ 4 5 Not Helpful Very Helpful
Source 3: www.howstuffworks.com	Gas and air mix in the engine cylinders.	The spark plugs light the gas and make an explosion that moves the cylinder.		Car engines run by many small explosions that turn parts that make them run.	1 2 3 ④ 5 Not Helpful Very Helpful
Summary of each subtopic or theme	Gas mixed with air in the engine's cylinders.	The battery and generator make electricity, which is used to ignite the gas in the cylinders.	Oil is used to keep metal parts running smoothly. The radiator helps cool the engine.	Engines in cars need many parts and systems in order to work.	

REFERENCES

Hoffman, J.V. (1992). Critical reading/thinking across the curriculum: Using I-charts to support learning. *Language Arts, 69*, 121–127.

Vygotsky, L.S. (1986). *Thought and language* (A. Kozalin, Trans.). Cambridge, MA: The MIT Press. (Original work published 1962)

CHAPTER 8

Learning-From-Text Guide

According to Singer and Donlan (1980), reading objectives can be divided into two categories: cognitive (objectives that inform the processing of the information) and affective (objectives that involve engagement with the processing). This notion is based on their belief that mastery of objectives at the lower levels of Bloom's taxonomy (1956) is necessary for mastery of objectives at higher levels. To aid students in meeting these objectives, Singer and Donlan designed the Learning-From-Text Guide in which they suggest that teachers have students analyze the content and examine questions according to the following three different levels:

1. Literal Level: explicit or directly stated factual information

2. Inferential Level: information that reflects significant relationships, inferences, and/or interpretations

3. Generalization/Evaluative Level: information that leads to generalizations and/or evaluations

While the first two categories address information related primarily to cognitive objectives, the third supports students' critical and affective or emotional responses with question stems such as, "How did you feel about...?"

Other study guides and strategy guides take an approach similar to Singer and Donlan's Learning-From-Text Guide. Herber's (1970) Levels-of-Comprehension Guide is similar to the Learning-From-Text Guide because they both lead the learner through the explicit, literal level of

Grade Levels
Primary, intermediate, middle, secondary

Subjects
Math, literature, content areas

Classroom Contexts
Individuals, small groups, whole class

information to the inferential level and, finally, to the evaluative or applied level. The significant difference between the two guides is that Herber recommends responding to statements whereas Singer and Donlan's original guide has students answer questions. In a later edition of their book, however, Singer and Donlan (1989) show guides that use statements as well as questions in an attempt to more fully foster inquiry and open discussion.

The more commonly used Question Answer Relationship, often referred to as the QAR, created by Raphael and McKinney (1983) is also similar to the Learning-From-Text Guide. In the QAR students are guided by the following categories (Raphael & Au, 2005): In the Book, In My Head, Right There, Think & Search, Author & Me, and On My Own. While the Learning-From-Text Guide asks teachers to divide the content into the three categories previously mentioned, the QAR divides the information into four main categories (Right There, Think & Search, Author & Me, and On My Own) and invites students to make comparisons among the types of questions asked within each category. Like the Learning-From-Text Guide, the QAR can be used at any grade level and across the curriculum. Figure 18 highlights some of the similarities of the two learning guides. When using the QAR, students should first master identifying and answering In the Book questions, which are similar to Singer and Donlan's first category, Literal Level: explicit or directly stated factual information. The QAR subcategories of In the Book, Right There, and Think & Search also fall under Singer and Donlan's first category. Once students feel confident answering these, they will move on to In My Head with the subcategories of Author & Me and On My Own. These categories of the QAR correspond with the second and third of the Learning-From-Text Guide, Inferential Level and Generalization/Evaluative Level. If students seem to be struggling with the ideas presented in the Learning-From-Text Guide, it may be a good idea to incorporate some of the vocabulary used in the QAR to alleviate any confusion.

Singer and Donlan (1989) recommend the following five-step process for constructing a Learning-From-Text Guide.

Step 1. Read the selection to determine the important content, remembering that students do not always have to be responsible for learning all of the information presented.

Step 2. Categorize the important information according to the three levels. It is usually easier to work backward—that is, start by constructing general or evaluative questions or statements, then decide on the inferences and interpretations that should support them, and finally list the explicit information that supports the inferences and generalizations.

Step 3. For the Literal Level of the guide, intersperse statements that appear in the text with a few that don't. The students must then

Figure 18. Comparison of Learning-From-Text Guide and QAR Questioning

Learning-From-Text Guide	QAR	Type of Text or Background Knowledge Used	Sample Question and Statement Beginnings
Literal Level	In the Book—Right There	Simple list, description, explanation, sequence	How many...? Who is...? Where are...? According to the passage...?
Inferential Level	In the Book—Think & Search	Simple list, description, explanation, sequence	The main idea of the passage.... Compare and contrast.... What caused...?
Generalization/ Evaluative Level	In My Head—Author & Me	Text-to-self, text-to-text, text-to-world connections	The author implies.... The passage suggests.... The speaker's attitude....
	In My Head—On My Own	Text-to-self, text-to-text, text-to-world connections	In your opinion...? Based on your experience...?

differentiate between the two by writing down the page numbers for statements that come from the text. If you use questions instead of statements, you can indicate the page numbers on which the answers appear.

Step 4. To construct the Inferential Level of the guide, it is important to develop questions or statements that will help students perceive the relationships among sentences and infer or interpret information to arrive at a conclusion. The following example illustrates how a question and a statement can be used to help students infer in this way.

Text passage: The strength, size, and ability to turn quickly help tugboats push and pull vessels of all sizes in, out, and around waterways.

Question: Why would boats need to be pushed and pulled around waterways?

Statement: Large boats may not be able to go slowly enough to move just a little bit; maybe the tug can give them a little push to get around the waterway.

In this example, students may infer that large boats and ships may have a difficult time maneuvering through waterways and that tugboats help them. The terms *strength*, *size*, and *ability to turn quickly* suggest that tugboats are small, strong boats. Those terms along with *push and pull vessels of all sizes* imply that they can move boats much larger than themselves.

Step 5. Like the Inferential Level, the Generalization/Evaluative Level of the guide can be constructed using either questions or statements. The following are examples of each for the previous text passage:

> *Statement*: Tugboats assist other vessels in difficult situations.
>
> *Question*: In what types of situations do you think tugboats are called upon to assist other vessels?

The statement allows the reader to offer the possibility that tugboats assist in times of danger as well as other times when there is no danger.

Figure 19 illustrates a Learning-From-Text Guide created for an intermediate-level science lesson (see page 180 in the Appendix for a reproducible version of this form). In this example, students are first instructed to answer the questions listed at the Literal Level; as previously suggested, we included similar vocabulary found in the QAR to clarify to students where they might find the answers. The guide provides an information index that helps them locate the page and paragraph in the text where the answer can be found. Next, students answer questions at the Inferential Level to help them read between the lines and combine the text-based information with their own prior knowledge. Finally, students extend the newly learned information to the higher level of Generalization/Evaluative by drawing a connection between content and their own beliefs on the topic. For example, Question C:1 in Figure 19 asks,

> Why and in what ways do you think the chipmunk plans ahead for winter?

A typical student response might be the following:

> If a chipmunk gets lazy and doesn't plan for winter, it can die. We learned that a lot of them die in their first year because they go hungry. Their food is not around in the cold months, so they have to plan ahead. Most chipmunks spend all day finding out how to get food and storing it away. They hunt for nuts and can put away as much as three bushels of nuts over a three day period.

As review, students are given three questions that are not already identified by their level, and the students must decide which level they

Figure 19. Intermediate-Level Learning-From-Text Guide for Science Lesson on Adaptations

Adaptations

Instructions: Read pages 42–51 in your science book, "What are some ways mammals are adaptable?" and answer the following questions with a partner.

A. Literal Level (answers found in the book)
1. What is an animal's environment? (p. 42, paragraph 1)
2. Provide examples of how the mule deer adapt to their environment. (p. 42, paragraph 2)
3. Why do the nightjar bird's feathers look like the forest floor? (p. 44, paragraph 2)
4. Why are the penguin's feathers waterproof? (p. 45, paragraph 1)
5. _____ are a body part on fish that help them get oxygen from water. (p. 46, paragraph 1)
6. What adaptation do catfish have that helps them find food? (p. 47, paragraph 1)
7. Give examples of how the desert iguana makes adaptations to live in its environment. (p. 49, paragraph 1)

B. Inferential Level (Think about what you read and search for the answer; it may be found as the main idea of a paragraph, or it may be why something was caused.)
1. How does camouflage help an animal stay safe from other animals that may want to hunt or harm it?
2. Hummingbirds and penguins are alike and different. Name a few similarities or differences.
3. Why do catfish need feelers to help them find food?
4. Why does a snake's mouth open wide to swallow food whole?

C. Generalization/Evaluative Level (Questions will be answered on your own by thinking and applying what you know about the topic.)
1. Why and in what ways do you think the chipmunk plans ahead for winter?
2. People adapt to their environment. Offer a few examples from your life experiences.
3. What color do you predict most desert animals are? Why do you predict that color?

Review: Think back to our class discussion on classifying questions. Below the following questions write the level (Literal, Inferential, or Generalization/Evaluative) each belongs to. After identifying each, turn to your partner and create at least one question for each level using the text you just read. These questions will be shared and charted with the class.

Part 1
1. What is camouflage?
   Type of Question:_____
2. Why does a rapid change in weather affect how quickly a snake moves?
   Type of Question: _____
3. In your opinion, why is it important for animals to adapt?
   Type of Question: _____

Part 2
Literal-Level Question: _____
_____
Inferential-Level Question:_____
_____
Generalization/Evaluative-Level Question:_____
_____

belong to. Then, when complete, they will work with a partner to create at least one question for each of the three levels.

In the example in Figure 20, secondary students were asked to complete a Learning-From-Text Guide similar to the example shown in Figure 19, but in this example the text is a history-based text on Buddhism, and the questions are not divided into the three separate categories (see page 181 in the Appendix for a reproducible version of this guide). Students begin by reading the selected passage and answering the questions. They will then be asked to get into pairs and compare their answers; if there are any discrepancies in answers, students must go back to the text and highlight where they gleaned their answer. Students are then asked to take the process one step further and list the questions in the accompanying diagram under the correct heading. When working with secondary students, it is important that they learn to identify the different types of questions on their own. After this activity has been completed once or twice with different texts, the teacher can ask the students to create their own Learning-From-Text Guides and switch with a partner; the partner would then have to answer the questions his or her partner created and check to make sure they are formulating the correct types of questions.

Tips for Diverse Learners

- Pair ELLs with another student or tutor who is proficient in English.
- Encourage the use of a word bank with pictures to support learning theme-based vocabulary.
- Create a chart to display different levels of questions with simple examples; use pictures or icons if possible.

REFERENCES

Bloom, B.S. (1956). *Taxonomy of educational objectives: The classification of educational goals*. New York: Addison Wesley.

Herber, H.L. (1970). *Teaching reading in the content areas*. Upper Saddle River, NJ: Prentice Hall.

Raphael, T.E., & Au, K.H. (2005). QAR: Enhancing comprehension and test taking across grades and content areas. *The Reading Teacher, 59*, 206–221.

Raphael, T.E., & McKinney, J. (1983). An examination of 5th and 8th grade children's question answering behavior: An instructional study in metacognition. *Journal of Reading Behavior, 15*, 67–86.

Singer, H., & Donlan, D. (1980). *Reading and learning from text*. Boston: Little, Brown.

Singer, H., & Donlan, D. (1989). *Reading and learning from text* (2nd ed.). Boston: Little, Brown.

Buddhism and Medieval Japan

Instructions: Read pages 19–21, "Buddhism and Medieval Japan," and answer the following questions on your own. When you have completed all the answers on this strategy guide, meet with a partner and compare your answers. If there are any discrepancies between your answers, go back to the text and highlight the information that supports your answer. If you find new information that discredits your answer, make the necessary changes so that it is correct.

When comparisons are complete, fill in the accompanying chart by copying each question under the appropriate heading. For example, if the question is a Literal-Level question and the answer is easily found straight from the text, then copy the question in the heading "Literal Level."

1. What shaped the ideas and institutions of the political and social structure of medieval Japan? (p. 19, paragraph 1)

2. Why do you think Buddhism shaped the categories of class and gender in Japan?

3. What do you find sacred in modern society?

4. Why did people pray to Buddhist divinities? (p. 20, paragraph 1)

5. Why would local deities, or kami, be integrated with mainstream deities?

6. What were the dates of the Kamakura period? (p. 20, paragraph 3)

7. What six schools of Buddhism were developed during the Kamakura period? (p. 20, paragraph 4)

8. Why were the older schools of Buddhism able to form powerful economic institutions, have large areas of land, and hold their own armed forces?

9. How do you find enlightenment in your own life?

10. What is Amida's vow? (p. 21, paragraph 2)

11. Why would choosing one form of ritual practice lead Buddhists into conflict with other religious believers as well as government officials?

Literal Level In the Book—Right There	**Inferential Level** In the Book— Think & Search	**Generalization/ Evaluative Level** In My Head—Author & Me In My Head—On My Own

Multiple-Source Research Guide

Today, students must gather and evaluate information from a wide variety of resources, including not only traditional print-based texts but also television and radio broadcasts, Internet pages, and online communications, to name a few. The Multiple-Source Research Guide (Wood, 1998; Wood & Beattie, 2004; Wood & Taylor, 2006) allows students to work collaboratively to find information and synthesize their understanding of a research topic based on information found in a collection of resources.

Before allowing students to begin their research, share a completed research assignment with the class. During this time, students are directed to make note of the way the piece is organized and how information is included in the text (both positive and negative examples are good illustrations to teach students how to write well). Students may also benefit from instruction on finding information, working with different types of resources, and citing their findings.

For the researching stage, assign students to heterogeneous groups of three to five students. Either give groups an assigned topic for study or allow them to choose a topic related to what is being studied. Give each student a blank copy of the Multiple-Source Research Guide (see page 182 in the Appendix for a reproducible version of the guide) and direct them to record relevant information and appropriate references. This will give students the material needed to complete the assignment and prepare them to create the bibliography.

Within each group, members decide who will pursue each type of source based on their knowledge and abilities; for example, students who

Grade Levels
Intermediate, middle, secondary

Subjects
Science, language arts, social studies, fine arts

Classroom Contexts
Whole class, small groups, pairs, individuals

Guiding Readers Through Text: Strategy Guides for New Times (2nd ed.) by Karen D. Wood, Diane Lapp, James Flood, and D. Bruce Taylor. © 2008 by the International Reading Association.

are adept at working with computers may choose to find information online while strong readers may prefer to search trade books. Flexible grouping may also be used to support struggling readers or English-language learners who require additional support. After conducting research, groups reassemble to share and organize information and decide how to proceed. Students take turns recording their findings on the Multiple-Source Research Guide and documenting their resources in a predetermined format. Group members must also proofread, edit, and create the final document.

In one intermediate-level class, two struggling readers, with one slightly more proficient than the other, were paired to provide assistance to each other as they sought out information on the topic of communicable diseases (see Figure 21). Each student located different sources of information, including a person-to-person interview with the school nurse. As is often the case with struggling readers, these two students found it beneficial to make charts and pictures of what they learned to help them remember and recall the information.

Figure 22 provides a Multiple-Source Research Guide for a secondary-level, social studies lesson related to a unit on the branches of the government. Instead of writing the information by hand, this example illustrates how students can work together to synthesize their findings, make revisions (even add clip art), and then submit the information from their sources electronically and in typewritten form.

Once students become comfortable with this procedure and can demonstrate that they are able to synthesize information from the sources, the activity can be restructured so that students are working in pairs and eventually independently. This is an excellent way to scaffold the process of synthesizing information that is so essential in the writing of research papers at any grade level.

Tips for Diverse Learners

- Thoroughly model and think aloud examples.
- Pair students who need extra scaffolding.
- Use pictorial information.
- Encourage labeling of key concepts.

REFERENCES

Wood, K.D. (1998). Flexible grouping and information literacy: A model of direct instruction. *North Carolina Middle Schools Association Journal*, 19(2), 1–5.

Wood, K.D., & Beattie, J. (2004). Meeting the literacy needs of students with ADHD in the middle school classroom. *Middle School Journal*, 35(3), 50–55.

Wood, K.D., & Taylor, D.B. (2006). *Literacy strategies across the subject areas: Process-oriented blackline masters for the K–12 classroom* (2nd ed.). Boston: Allyn & Bacon.

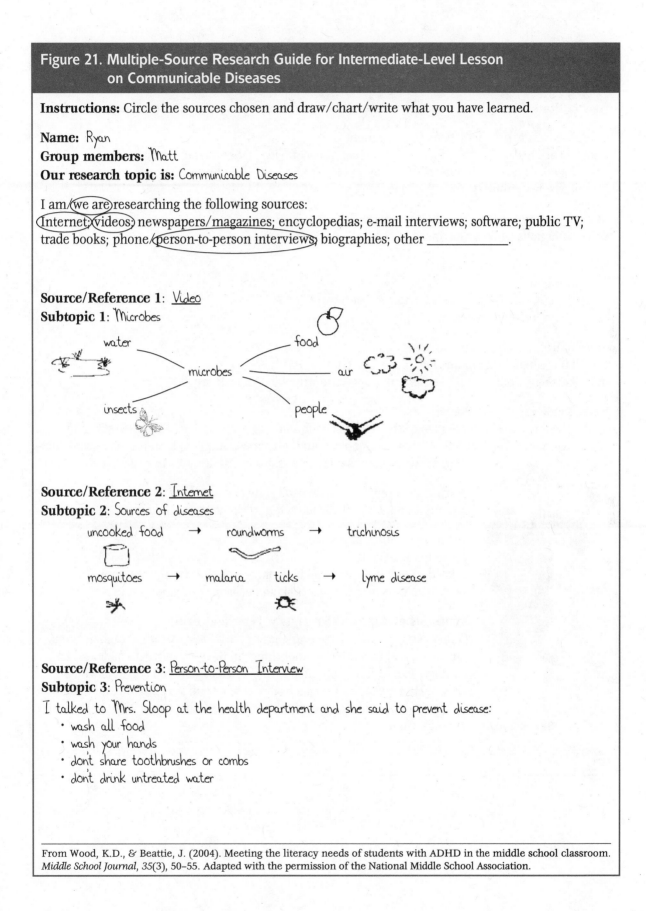

Figure 21. Multiple-Source Research Guide for Intermediate-Level Lesson on Communicable Diseases

Instructions: Circle the sources chosen and draw/chart/write what you have learned.

Name: Ryan
Group members: Matt
Our research topic is: Communicable Diseases

I am/(we are) researching the following sources:
(Internet)(videos;) newspapers/magazines; encyclopedias; e-mail interviews; software; public TV; trade books; phone/(person-to-person interviews;) biographies; other _____.

Source/Reference 1: Video
Subtopic 1: Microbes

water — food — air — people — insects → microbes

Source/Reference 2: Internet
Subtopic 2: Sources of diseases

uncooked food → roundworms → trichinosis

mosquitoes → malaria   ticks → lyme disease

Source/Reference 3: Person-to-Person Interview
Subtopic 3: Prevention

I talked to Mrs. Sloop at the health department and she said to prevent disease:
- wash all food
- wash your hands
- don't share toothbrushes or combs
- don't drink untreated water

From Wood, K.D., & Beattie, J. (2004). Meeting the literacy needs of students with ADHD in the middle school classroom. *Middle School Journal, 35*(3), 50–55. Adapted with the permission of the National Middle School Association.

Instructions: Circle the sources chosen and draw/chart/write what you have learned.

Our research topic: Branches of Government
I am/we are researching the following sources: Internet, videos; newspapers/magazines; encyclopedias, e-mail interviews; software; public TV, trade books, phone/person-to-person interviews; biographies; other Textbook, our senator

Source/Reference 1: Government website (Sasha)
www.whitehouse.gov/government/exec.html

Subtopic 1: Executive Branch
The president
He is the commander in chief of the armed forces.
He oversees other government people.

Source/Reference 2: Our senator (Peter)
E-mail our senator, Elizabeth Dole.
dole.senate.gov/index.cfm?FuseAction=ContactInformation.ContactForm

Subtopic 2: Legislative Branch
Senator Dole is one of our Senators. She said that each state has senators and senators that go to Washington and vote on the laws that the people from their state want. People in the states vote for their favorite congressman or senator and that's how they get elected.

Source/Reference 3: Trade book (Lily and Juan)
The Supreme Court and the Judicial Branch by Bryon Giddens-White

Subtopic 3: Judicial Branch
The Supreme Court
They decide if laws are legal by looking at past laws and the constitution.
They help pass new laws by making decisions on important cases.

Synthesis of Sources: (Sasha, Lily, Peter, and Juan)
Our government has three branches or parts. The executive branch is the president, and he oversees other things in the government and leads the military. The legislative branch is the congressmen and senators who are elected by the people from each state. They go to Washington and make the laws. The judicial branch is the courts and especially the Supreme Court where they help make the laws and decide on important cases.

Created by graduate student Aimee Grace Alder of the University of North Carolina at Charlotte, USA. Reprinted with permission.

CHAPTER 10

Point-of-View Guide

In the Point-of-View Guide (described in Buehl, 2001; Wood, 1988, 1991; Wood & Harmon, 2001), questions are presented in an interview format to allow students to gain different perspectives on the events described in both traditional printed selections and—as with all of the guides—nontraditional print sources as well. This format requires students to contribute their own experiences as they assume the role of various characters, thereby enhancing their recall and comprehension skills.

The purpose of the Point-of-View Guide is threefold. First, it helps develop the important skill of mental elaboration, as it requires the students to add their own information as they read. Second, it encourages the skill of mental recitation—the most powerful study technique known to psychologists (Pauk, 1974)—by having students put new information in their own words. Third, it helps students learn the content of the selection. We have seen teachers use the Point-of-View Guide with all grade levels, including the primary grades. When modeled effectively, first- and second-grade students enjoy taking on the perspective of a "very hungry caterpillar," a "rainbow fish," or even America's first president.

Because students are unlikely to have encountered this activity before, it will be necessary to model the process thoroughly at the outset. Instruct the students to write their responses in the first-person point of view, elaborating whenever possible with information from their experiences. Use examples to show how this type of response differs from typical textbook-like responses. For a text passage on U.S. history, for instance, we've provided a sample question and answer in each style.

> *Text Passage*: Even on the battlefield, the lack of American unity was visible. At the Battle of Niagara, a group of New York soldiers, refusing to leave New York, stood and watched their outnumbered comrades across the river being killed.

Grade Levels
Primary, intermediate, middle, secondary

Subjects
Reading/language arts, social studies, science, fine arts

Classroom Contexts
Individuals, small groups, whole class, tutoring sessions

Guiding Readers Through Text: Strategy Guides for New Times (2nd ed.) by Karen D. Wood, Diane Lapp, James Flood, and D. Bruce Taylor. © 2008 by the International Reading Association.

A textbook may offer the following basic questions based on this passage—"Was America ready to fight? Why or why not?" In this context, students likely will provide an answer resembling the following:

No, because at the Battle of Niagara, a group of New York soldiers, refusing to leave New York, stood and watched their outnumbered comrades across the river being killed.

However, unlike the textbook-style question, an interview question for this passage might read, "Put yourself in the place of a person living in the United States in the early 1800s. In your opinion, were the Americans ready to fight? Explain why you feel this way." A student response might look like the following:

No, we weren't ready to fight. Some of us, the war hawks, wanted war. Others didn't. Some New Yorkers at the Battle of Niagara stood by as their friends got killed. We lacked unity. We didn't even have muskets and other equipment. Some of us had to use our own guns or borrow some.

In the first example, the student has used the question stem as a starting point and has copied the remainder of the information directly from the textbook. This sort of text-based response typifies the answers often given in a classroom. In contrast, notice how the interview question allows for elaboration, inferential thinking, and speculation. Note also how the interview format frees students to use less stilted, more natural language. Therefore, to get the most out of this exercise, students should be encouraged to respond in dialogue format whenever possible.

Continue to model passages to explain the concept of taking on another's perspective until students fully understand this interviewing method. It is suggested that teachers first "think aloud" responses to one of the passages and then encourage the class to do the same for a subsequent example. Then they can work in small groups or pairs to discuss their thinking for other illustrations before being asked to complete the guide designed for the topic under study. The following are various modeling examples of the interview format, organized by subject matter.

Science Text Passage: A crocodile can grow to a length of 20 feet, weigh half a ton, and tackle a 900-pound buffalo that wanders past at lunchtime. A crocodile can stay under water for $2\frac{1}{2}$ hours without a breath of air by slowing his heartbeat and going into semihibernation. He can outrun a man in a 100-yard dash, although there is no record of any such footrace.

Question: Imagine that you are a crocodile swimming down the Zambezi River in Africa. Tell us about yourself and what you are thinking as a tourist wades in the waters nearby.

Language Arts Text Passage: At a little one-room, mountain schoolhouse, the big boys in the upper grades enjoyed driving off school teachers. Finally, the school had to close because there was no teacher. A few weeks later, however, a pale, thin, harmless-looking fellow showed up to ask about the teaching job. He was told what he was up against.

Question: You are the teacher who has just shown up for the job. What training have you had? Describe your plans for this class.

Social Studies Text Passage: Britain and France responded to the U.S. trade laws by capturing American merchant ships and seizing their cargoes. Often the British took American sailors and forced them to join the British navy. Although the trade laws hurt France and Britain, they probably hurt the United States more. Shipping businesses in New York, Boston, and other large port cities nearly collapsed.

Question: As a merchant in a coastal town, tell what is happening to your business and why it is doing so poorly.

Once students understand how to use the interview format, you can present them with a Point-of-View Guide to help guide their reading of a text and deepen and extend their understanding. Figure 23 pictures a Point-of-View Guide for an intermediate-level text selection on the War of 1812. To give the students a fuller understanding of events from a variety of perspectives, the guide asks them to take on a number of different roles. Similarly, Figure 24 illustrates how this type of guide can be used with a U.S. history lesson on the World War II era at the secondary level. In this case the student assumes the perspective of a person living in the United States after 1941. To deepen their understanding, the teacher has asked that they consult additional sources related to the issues and events of the times.

Related to this topic but in the content area of English language arts, the guide shown in Figure 25 was designed in an intermediate-level reading methods class by preservice teacher Katie Hunter (now a teacher in Cabarrus County Schools, North Carolina, USA) to accompany chapter 5 of Lois Lowry's (1998) novel *Number the Stars*. Students are asked to take on the role of Annemarie Johansen and describe in "her" words her thoughts, emotions, and reactions as she experiences growing up during World War II. With the face of the main character forming the basis of the guide, students are motivated to step into Annemarie's world and read the chapter from her perspective.

In another English language arts Point-of-View Guide, Figure 26 illustrates a Point-of-View Guide designed for Rudyard Kipling's (2004) *Rikki-Tikki-Tavi* by literacy specialist Susan Avett and implemented in the classroom by middle school language arts teacher Ross Crandell (Wood & Harmon, 2001). The guide reads like an interview script a media reporter might use as students are asked to describe what "they" look like as they take on the role of "Mr. Tavi." Then they are asked how they felt when they first met "Nag" and learned of the plot between Nag and Nagaina to kill the people with whom Rikki-Tikki-Tavi lived. Because students may not be familiar with characteristics of the animals in this story, the teacher has included an assignment to look up information about these animals from other sources before they take on the perspective of the main character.

Figure 23. Point-of-View Guide for Intermediate-Level Lesson on the War of 1812

Chapter 11: The War of 1812

You are about to be interviewed as if you were a person living in the United States in the early 1800s. Be sure to consult some other sources as well as your text as you describe your reactions to each of the events discussed next.

Planting the Seeds of War (p. 285)
1. As a merchant in a coastal town, tell why your business is doing poorly.
   The British had a blockade on our ports so no ships could come or go to trade.

The War Debate (pp. 285–87)
2. Explain why you decided to become a war hawk. Who was your leader?
   Because the British were kidnapping our guys and making them fight on their side and also they were stopping us from trading. We followed John Randolph.

3. Tell why many of your fellow townspeople lowered their flags to half mast. What else did they do?
   They did that in support of our soldiers and they stopped using stuff made by the British too.

4. What was the reaction of Great Britain to you and your people at that time?
   They were angry and that was part of the reason they started pressing or kidnapping our people for their navy, to help them fight the French.

5. In your opinion, is America ready to fight? Explain why you feel this way.
   Yeah, we are. We already beat the British once, and they are having to fight two different countries so they will be weaker.

Perry's Victory (p. 287)
6. In what ways were your predictions either correct or incorrect about Americans' readiness to fight this war?
   I was right 'cause we beat the British at the Battle of Lake Erie and that helped us win other battles 'cause we had control of the lake.

7. Tell about your experiences under Captain Perry's command.
   It was hard. We had to move all of the cannons across the sandbar by hand to block off the British in their fort. We also had to tow boats up the Niagara River, which was really tough.

Death of Tecumseh (p. 288)
8. Mr. Harrison, describe what really happened near the Thames River in Canada.
   Well, Proctor, the British General was scared of us and would not fight. This made his own soldiers not want to fight hard for him. Finally he decided to. But when we started fighting his cannons wouldn't fire so the British gave up and ran away. Tecumseh stayed to fight but we beat them in the end 'cause he only had like 500 guys left.

(continued)

---

9. What was Richard Johnson's role in that battle?

He led the horse charge that finally broke the Indians' fighting line, and he might have been the one to kill Tecumseh.

10. Now, what are your future plans?

I plan to move out to the Ohio Territory and get some land.

Death of the Creek Confederacy (p. 288)

11. Explain how your people, the Cherokees, actually helped the United States.

We joined with the Americans to fight the Creeks and their allies, the British, and we beat them at the Battle of Horseshoe Bend.

12. Tell us about your leader.

Our leader was John Coffee, who led a brigade of Indians and free African Americans. He was a great leader who fought in most of the battles in the Creek War and the War of 1812 and was even wounded.

British Invasion (pp. 288–90)

13. As a British soldier, what happened when you got to Washington, DC?

We were given strict orders to loot and burn only the government buildings since we wanted to destroy the government, but not the civilians or their houses.

14. You headed to Fort McHenry after DC; what was the outcome?

We tried to bomb the Americans in Fort McHenry, which was guarding the harbor of Baltimore. After 25 hours of bombing we could still see the American flag flying over the fort and knew we couldn't beat them. Francis Scott Key was watching that battle and he described it in a poem that is the American national anthem, "The Star Spangled Banner."

15. General Jackson, it's your turn. Tell about your army and how you defeated the British of New Orleans.

When I got the news that the British were coming out to attack New Orleans I knew we weren't ready 'cause we didn't have our cannons in position yet. So I attacked the British in their camp to give my other soldiers more time to get ready. We beat the British really badly, mostly because they forgot to bring their ladders so they could get over the dirt walls we had made.

The Treaty of Ghent (p. 290)

16. We will end our interview with some final observations from the merchant questioned earlier. We will give you some names and people. Tell how they fare now that the war is over: the British, the Indians, the United States, Harrison, Jackson.

The British lost and their influence over America was mostly over. Things just got worse for the Indians as the Americans began to drive them off their land. The United States began to become more confident as a new nation. Andrew Jackson was so popular after the Battle of New Orleans that he was elected president.

Adapted from Wood, K.D. (1988). Guiding students through informational text. *The Reading Teacher, 41*, 912–920. Adapted with the permission of the International Reading Association.

America After 1941

You are about to be interviewed as if you were a person living in the United States after 1941. Be sure to consult some other sources as well as your text as you describe your reactions to each of the events discussed next. In addition to your textbook, you will need to seek out some additional sources as you take on the perspective of the individuals of this era in American history.

America's Huge War Needs (pp. 617–18)

1. As a worker in a U.S. defense plant, tell what effect the War Production Board has had on you, your coworkers, and the soldiers overseas.

    Since Roosevelt started up the War Production Board in 1942, we have been busy every minute. We're building twice as many tanks and supplies as ever before. We work like crazy—a lot of overtime, too. The troops overseas ought to be happy though. We're producing more supplies and weapons than all our enemies put together! en.wikipedia.org/wiki/War_Production_Board

Americans Go Back to Work (p. 618)

2. As one of the leaders in a national labor union, what is your reaction to the need for war supplies? Be sure to consult the "labor union" section of the following source in addition to your textbook: eh.net/encyclopedia/article/tassava.WWII

    I am excited about the new production that will help with all the poor business we have had lately due to the Depression, and I am ready to do my patriotic duty, help cheer on my workers, and collect the union dues. We are just one of many new labor unions that are springing up in the U.S. now that they have changed the rules.

3. As a farmer, tell how your life has changed from the Depression days to the present days of wartime.

    My sons are going off to fight in the war, and my crops are much more in demand as the economy is starting to pick up.

Opportunities for Blacks (pp. 618–19)
As a black person from the South:

4. Tell why you and others moved to the northeastern and midwestern sections of the United States.

    I moved because I knew I could find work in a factory and I thought I would face less discrimination than in the South.

5. Describe the effect of Hitler's racist doctrine on your situation at home.

    It made things hard in some areas where groups like the KKK agreed with what Hitler was saying.

6. Tell why Executive Order 8802 was important to you. See also the actual Executive Order: www.eeoc.gov/abouteeoc/35th/thelaw/eo-8802.html

    This was so important because it was the first federal law ever that prohibited discrimination by race in businesses that were working for national defense. It was also the first law ever passed that tried to promote equal opportunity.

Adapted from Wood, K.D., Lapp, D., & Flood, J. (1992). *Guiding readers through text: A review of study guides* (p. 13). Newark, DE: International Reading Association. Reprinted with the permission of the International Reading Association.

Figure 25. Point-of-View Guide for Lois Lowry's *Number the Stars*

Name: _____

Number the Stars
Point of View Study Guide
Chapter 5: Who is the Dark-Haired One?

After reading Chapter 5, you are now Annemaire Johansen. In your journal, describe your thoughts, emotions, and reactions to the chapter.
(Be sure to answer the following questions in Annemaire's point of view.)

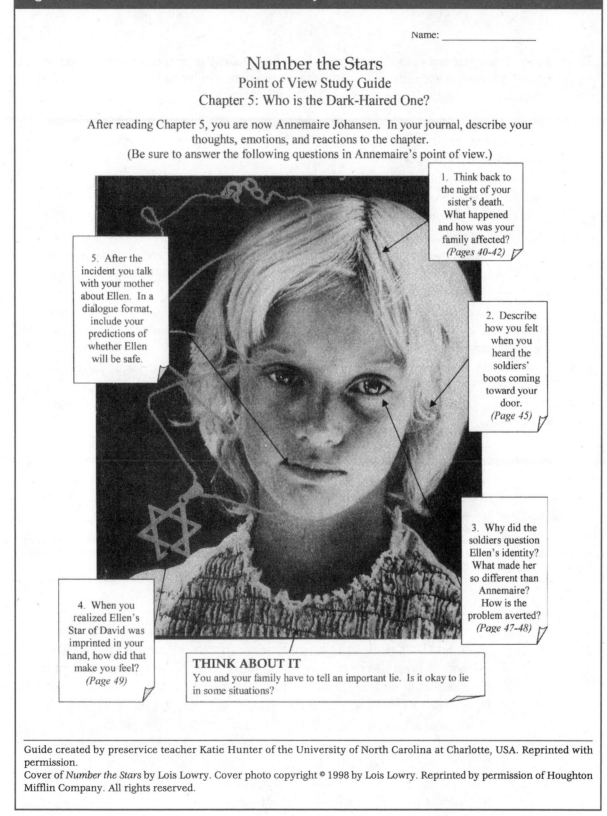

1. Think back to the night of your sister's death. What happened and how was your family affected? *(Pages 40-42)*

5. After the incident you talk with your mother about Ellen. In a dialogue format, include your predictions of whether Ellen will be safe.

2. Describe how you felt when you heard the soldiers' boots coming toward your door. *(Page 45)*

3. Why did the soldiers question Ellen's identity? What made her so different than Annemaire? How is the problem averted? *(Page 47-48)*

4. When you realized Ellen's Star of David was imprinted in your hand, how did that make you feel? *(Page 49)*

THINK ABOUT IT
You and your family have to tell an important lie. Is it okay to lie in some situations?

Figure 26. Point-of-View Guide for Rudyard Kipling's *Rikki-Tikki-Tavi*

Rikki-Tikki-Tavi

This story involves a number of interesting animals. Before reading, go to some online sources to find out more information about the following animals: mongoose, tailor bird, and cobra. This will help you as you as take on the perspective of Rikki-Tikki-Tavi.

1. Since we are not there in person to see you ourselves, please, Mr. Tavi, tell us what you look like?

   I have golden fur and a cute nose and a bushy tail. Sometimes when I am very angry my black eyes turn bright red. Well, that's pretty much it.

2. Mr. Tavi, how did you come to live with Teddy's family after all?

   A summer flood washed me out of my burrow where I lived with my family. I was washed into a ditch. Then I awoke and saw these nice people. They dried me off and warmed me up.

3. What was your first night in a strange place like?

   It was very different. I was really curious. I began to explore the house after the people went to sleep. I went all through the house and decided that if I stayed here I could learn many things.

4. How did you feel the first time you saw Nag? Describe Nag for us.

   The first time I saw Nag I was scared. I saw how everyone in the garden was afraid of him, so I was careful. But after I saw him and studied him for a bit I noticed he was a snake, and I wasn't afraid anymore because I don't get afraid often, and I know mongooses are supposed to kill snakes.

5. What was your reaction when you heard Nag and Nagaina plotting to kill the people you live with?

   I was so furious. But I knew I would have to be calm. If they killed the family I lived with, then I wouldn't have a home and would have to leave. But I was patient and I ended up saving them and killing Nag.

6. It must have been a very tense moment when you found Nagaina ready to strike at Teddy. How did you manage to divert her attention?

   I had to make a deal with her. It was very tense, but I thought that since her husband was dead, if she had only one baby left she would be very careful of it. I used the fact that I had the egg to distract her and turn her attention, then the family would be safe.

Created by literacy specialist Susan Avett. Originally published in Wood, K.D., & Harmon, J.M. (2001). *Strategies for integrating reading and writing in middle and high school classrooms* (p. 91). Westerville, OH: National Middle School Association. Reprinted with the permission of the National Middle School Association.

The Point-of-View Guide can be used in other subject areas and grade levels as well. In science, for example, students could describe dissection from the perspective of a nematode, photosynthesis from the perspective of a plant, or an eruption from the point of view of a volcano. In a literature class, students can readily assume the roles and emotions of the characters in a selection. One teacher found the point-of-view approach useful in teaching primary students about the meeting of cultures in colonial America. After reading aloud a story about Thanksgiving, the teacher had students write a brief account of their lives as either a pilgrim or a Native American.

Tips for Diverse Learners

- Pair ELL students with English-speaking students.
- Model, demonstrate, and think aloud sample responses.
- Use pictures as a prompt and encourage students to guess at the dialogue.

REFERENCES

Buehl, D. (2001). *Classroom strategies for interactive learning* (2nd ed.). Newark, DE: International Reading Association.

Pauk, W. (1974). *How to study in college* (2nd ed.). Boston: Houghton Mifflin.

Wood, K.D. (1988). Guiding students through informational text. *The Reading Teacher, 41,* 912–920.

Wood, K.D. (1991). Changing perspective to improve comprehension. *Middle School Journal, 22*(3), 52–56.

Wood, K.D., & Harmon, J.M. (2001). *Strategies for integrating reading and writing in middle and high school classrooms.* Westerville, OH: National Middle School Association.

Wood, K.D., Lapp, D., & Flood, J. (1992). *Guiding readers through text: A review of study guides.* Newark, DE: International Reading Association.

LITERATURE CITED

Kipling, R. (2004). *Rikki-Tikki-Tavi.* New York: HarperTrophy.

Lowry, L. (1998). *Number the stars.* Boston: Houghton Mifflin.

PART IV

Statement Guides

G uides in this section give teachers the opportunity to witness their students' cognitive growth. The guides allow teachers to see where students are in their thinking during the prereading stage, and they enable teachers to eavesdrop on students' new learning, as reflected in discussions, during the postreading stage. Students must use their prior knowledge and experience to predict if each statement is true or false and engage in a discussion with their peers. The statements are used as their guide while reading, listening to, or viewing the content. Then they are asked to return to the statements to determine if they have changed their mind or broadened their view, substantiating their responses with support from the content sources.

CHAPTER 11

Anticipation Guide

Grade Levels
Primary, intermediate, middle, secondary

Subjects
Reading/language arts, social studies, science, math, fine arts

Classroom Contexts
Pairs, small groups, whole class

The idea of presenting a series of statements to guide students' responses before, during, and after reading a selection has been discussed extensively in the professional literature on content area instruction. Among the first to use such statements was Herber (1970), who included them in his Reasoning Guide, a teacher-developed strategy for eliciting analytical thinking and discussion about topics under study. Readence, Bean, and Baldwin (1981); Bean, Readence, and Baldwin (2008); and Merkley (1996–1997) describe the Anticipation (or Reaction) Guide and Nichols (1983) the Prediction Guide, which are similar in purpose and format in that they use carefully designed statements to stimulate thinking and activate prior knowledge. Guides of this type are advocated in the professional literature as a means to encourage students' discussion and thinking on a topic before reading, as a way to help students selectively attend to information during reading, and as a way to continue and expand their discussion after reading (Alvermann & Phelps, 2005; Vacca & Vacca, 2008). We have decided to use the term *Anticipation Guide* because of the extensive research through the years on the need to elicit students' prior knowledge on a topic before reading a selection (Gambrell, Morrow, & Pressley, 2007), asking students to use what they already know about a topic in order to *anticipate* the content of the information sources to follow.

We recommend that the teacher distribute a blank copy of the guide to each student or display the guide on an overhead or computer projector for whole-class access. (We like to use an overhead as well as hand out a printed blank copy to each student.) Then, working in pairs, have the students take turns reading each statement aloud to their partner. They must discuss why they either agree or disagree with the statement, drawing from their prior knowledge, experiences, or even predictions about the content to follow. This substantiation part is

Guiding Readers Through Text: Strategy Guides for New Times (2nd ed.) by Karen D. Wood, Diane Lapp, James Flood, and D. Bruce Taylor. © 2008 by the International Reading Association.

essential and what makes the Anticipation Guide a true tool for promoting discussion. After the pairs of students have completed their responses, engage in a whole-class discussion of the responses by marking in the "Before" column on the overhead. One way to begin this is to ask for a volunteer to read each statement, and after the student reads the statement say something like,

> How many people agreed with this statement? Raise your hand. How many disagreed? If you agreed with the statement, tell why you answered that way. If you disagreed with the statement, explain your thinking. Now, let's read the content using these statements as our guide. We will return to the statements afterward to see if you have broadened your view or changed your mind about your original answers.

If there is sufficient time, you may also want to use a similar format in the postreading stage. Have students discuss what they have learned in pairs, mark as appropriate in the "After" column, and then engage in a whole-class discussion.

Anticipation Guides can be used with all subject matter at all grade levels. They can also be used with all types of traditional printed material including textbooks, trade books, chapters, newspaper and magazine articles, as well as nontraditional printed material obtained through the Internet. Anticipation Guides are also appropriate for nonprint sources such as video, virtual tours, lectures from an outside speaker, field trips, and so on. Anticipation Guides are not limited to use with a single text but can also be used to frame an entire thematic unit, lesson, chapter, or any other comprehensive source.

The Anticipation Guide is a particularly effective strategy guide to use with younger students. Some teachers with whom we have worked have used them successfully with kindergarten and even preschool students. One preschool teacher we know developed an example of a guide on Eric Carle's (1994) *The Very Hungry Caterpillar*. As is illustrated in Figure 27, she used a smiling face to indicate agreement and a frowning face to indicate disagreement (see page 183 in the Appendix for a reproducible version of this guide). The teacher read each statement to the students while pointing to each word in the sentences, and then asked the students to talk over in their groups what they thought. The sample responses included in Figure 27 are representative of those group discussions. After reading the story to the students, they returned to the guide and related some details from the story, expressing surprise and excitement at the new information they had learned. Then, the teacher showed the students two related websites. One was author Eric Carle's official website at www.eric-carle.com and the other was a website about the habits of real caterpillars to differentiate between the caterpillar in the story and those in real life.

The Very Hungry Caterpillar
By: Eric Carle

BEFORE	STATEMENT	AFTER
🙂 ☹️	1. Caterpillars start as eggs. *No, just chickens, silly.*	🙂 ☹️
🙂 ☹️	2. Caterpillars turn into butterflies. *I don't think this is true.*	🙂 ☹️
🙂 ☹️	3. Caterpillars never eat sausage. *Caterpillars don't eat sausage. They eat leaves.*	🙂 ☹️
🙂 ☹️	4. Eating can give you a stomachache. *Yes, I had that happen to me.*	🙂 ☹️
🙂 ☹️	5. Caterpillars eat more each day. *I don't think this is true. They eat the same.*	🙂 ☹️

In another example, the Anticipation Guide in Figure 28 was used to begin a first-grade science unit on plants (see page 184 in the Appendix for a reproducible version of this guide). Before beginning the unit, the teacher read each statement with the class and then asked the students to pair up and discuss their reactions. Imagine the comments of some first graders to statement number 3: "People eat plants." Comments were overheard, such as "Nobody would want to eat a plant" and "That is not true because people do not eat flowers or leaves." Over the next six weeks, students read stories and informational text selections, listened to read-alouds, watched a video, grew their own plants from seeds, and took a virtual tour of a nursery. The teacher returned to the guide at the conclusion of the unit as a form of review and synthesis. This time, the students' comments included recollections from all of the varied sources of information they encountered in the unit. The guide served as a form of assessment, demonstrating the growth of their knowledge from the beginning of the unit.

Figure 29 features an Anticipation Guide that frames the reading of Gary Soto's (1990) short story "Seventh Grade," which appears in a

Figure 28. Anticipation Guide for First-Grade Science Unit on Plants

Topic: Plants

Directions: React to the following statements by placing a plus (+) in the left column if you agree or a minus (–) if you disagree.

BEFORE	STATEMENT	AFTER
–	1. A seed can grow into a tree. *No way, a seed maybe can become a plant, but not a tree.*	
+	2. Trees have many uses. *They are for shade and look pretty around houses and streets.*	
–	3. People eat plants. *No, that is not true because people do not eat flowers or leaves.*	
–	4. Plants have needs like people have needs. *They need water, but that's about it.*	
+	5. Plants help people. *Well, they look pretty in a garden.*	
–	6. Plants are alive. *Plants aren't really alive.*	

Figure 29. Anticipation Guide for Gary Soto's "Seventh Grade"

Topic/Title: "Seventh Grade" by Gary Soto

Directions: Take turns reading each of these statements with your partner. In the "Before" column, put a plus (+) if you agree with the statement or a minus (–) if you disagree. Make sure you justify your reactions with personal experiences, ideas, events, or analogies. After reading, return to the statements by marking what the story says and indicate in the "After" column if you have changed your mind or broadened your views.

BEFORE	STATEMENT	AFTER	
		Author	You
	1. When you like someone, you sometimes do unusual things. The story is about Victor who has a crush on Teresa and does crazy things to get her to notice him.		+
	2. Sometimes people go to extremes to make a good impression. Victor was acting like he could speak French in class to impress Teresa.		+
	3. Being yourself always pays off in the end. At some point, she is going to find out that he doesn't know French, maybe when they try to do homework together. Then, she will drop him!		+
	4. Others can always see through you if you are not being yourself. On the last page of the story, it was obvious that the French teacher, Mr. Buehler, knew he was speaking "gibberish," but he didn't give it away. Probably the rest of the kids in the class didn't know.		–

literature anthology used in a middle school classroom (see page 185 in the Appendix for a reproducible version of this guide). The statements in this guide get students to think about what it is like on the first day of school at a new grade level and how they or other students might try to make and impress new friends. As such, the statements reflect the major theme of Soto's story that we do indeed often go to great lengths to impress new friends as the young boy (Victor) in this story fakes his facility with the French language in order to impress a girl in his class (Teresa). Note that the sample student responses for this guide are from the postreading stage, after the students had read the story. Students worked in pairs to discuss their responses and then they shared their thinking with the entire class, indicating where they found support for their answers. Notice how this guide asks students to tell what they think the author is trying to say by including a third column. This can lead the way to a discussion comparing and contrasting the students' thoughts with the author's message.

Tips for Diverse Learners

- Pair ELL students with English-speaking students.
- Provide assistance during reading or listening activity.
- Use pictures and graphics and label as needed.

REFERENCES

Alvermann, D.E., & Phelps, S.F. (2005). *Content reading and literacy: Succeeding in today's diverse classrooms* (4th ed.). Boston: Allyn & Bacon.

Bean, T.W., Readence, J.E., & Baldwin, R.S. (2008). *Content area literacy: An integrated approach* (9th ed.). Dubuque, IA: Kendall/Hunt.

Gambrell, L.B., Morrow, L.M., & Pressley, M. (Eds.). (2007). *Best practices in literacy instruction* (3rd ed.). New York: Guilford.

Herber, H.L. (1970). *Teaching reading in the content areas.* Upper Saddle River, NJ: Prentice Hall.

Merkley, D.J. (1996–1997). Modified anticipation guide. *The Reading Teacher, 50,* 365–368.

Nichols, J.N. (1983). Using prediction to increase content area interest and understanding. *Journal of Reading, 27,* 225–228.

Readence, J.E., Bean, T.W., & Baldwin, R.S. (1981). *Content area reading: An integrated approach.* Dubuque, IA: Kendall/Hunt.

Vacca, R.T., & Vacca, J.A.L. (2008). *Content area reading: Literacy and learning across the curriculum* (9th ed.). Boston: Allyn & Bacon.

LITERATURE CITED

Carle, E. (1994). *The very hungry caterpillar.* New York: Philomel Books.

Soto, G. (1990). Seventh grade. In G. Soto, *Baseball in April and other stories* (pp. 52–59). New York: Odyssey Books.

CHAPTER 12

Extended Anticipation Guide

Duffelmeyer and Baum (1992) modified the Anticipation Guide (see chapter 11) to create what they called the Extended Anticipation Guide (Duffelmeyer, Baum, & Merkley, 1987). The major difference between the Anticipation Guide (described by Merkley, 1996–1997; Readence, Bean, & Baldwin, 1981) and the modified Extended Anticipation Guide created by Duffelmeyer and his colleagues is the addition of a section in which students must provide written justification of their thinking. The Extended Anticipation Guide is especially appropriate for all grade levels beyond the primary grades because of the independent writing required. Like the Anticipation Guide, the Extended Anticipation Guide begins in the prereading stage of a lesson as students predict and discuss the statements. The guide can then be used during reading as students look for content related to the statements, and then used in the postreading stage with the teacher and class sharing their written responses. Teachers can adapt the original format to include online assignments, websites, viewing experiences, field trips, experiments, read-alouds, lectures, and demonstrations (see Wood, 2000; Wood & Harmon, 2001).

The teacher begins by introducing the guide before reading as a means of stimulating discussion and finding out what students already know about a topic. It may be necessary for the teacher to model think-aloud examples of responses to one or more of the statements to illustrate the type of thinking that goes into a response to a statement since this may be a new activity for the students. Then the students are assigned to

Grade Levels
Intermediate, middle, secondary

Subjects
Reading/language arts, social studies, science, fine arts

Classroom Contexts
Individuals, small groups, whole class, tutoring sessions

Guiding Readers Through Text: Strategy Guides for New Times (2nd ed.) by Karen D. Wood, Diane Lapp, James Flood, and D. Bruce Taylor. © 2008 by the International Reading Association.

pairs (or small heterogeneous groups) to engage in a discussion about each statement.

The Extended Anticipation Guide shown in Figure 30 is for an intermediate-level class getting ready to read the book *Sharks* by Carol Baldwin (2003) to supplement their science unit on ocean life. This guide was designed by Schuyler Quinley, Alicia Jones, Jessica Bridges, and Shannon Burpeau, preservice teachers from the University of North Carolina at Charlotte, for an undergraduate reading methods class. The first two columns of the guide require that the students circle the "fin" indicating whether they agree or disagree with the statement in the middle section. The sample responses shown in Figure 30 represent student thinking and responding before they have consulted the content assigned for this lesson. It is imperative that students not just mark *agree* or *disagree* but that they also discuss with their partner why they responded in a particular manner, substantiating and justifying their thinking.

Next, students are instructed to read the selection, using the statements in the middle column to guide their reading. If desired, they can make mental or written notes of related content as they read. After their reading of the selection, they go to the next agree and disagree columns and mark the fin that corresponds with the newly learned content. The last column requires that they "Justify" and find support in the text for their responses, rewriting in their own words and the words of the text what the selection says about the concepts reflected in the statements. After a whole-class discussion of the responses in the justification section of the guide, students are asked to work in pairs and research various websites. With this newly learned information, they are to create posters of ways to save the shark population to be presented and displayed in class.

Teachers in our classes have adapted the Extended Anticipation Guide in many different ways. One secondary school teacher, Aimee Alder, had students seek out all of their answers from online sources. As shown in Figure 31, the students in a social studies class were asked to find out information on the student protests in China in Tiananmen Square, a topic about which they had just started reading in class (see page 186 in the Appendix for a reproducible version of this guide).

From our experiences in demonstrating the Extended Anticipation Guide in classrooms, we've learned that it is best to preassign students to pairs or small groups to complete the guides. Students can take turns reading each of the statements aloud and then share their reactions by agreeing or disagreeing with them. They must substantiate their responses by citing one or more reasons, examples, hypotheses, or anecdotes. Without this all-important substantiation step, the task resembles a true–false exercise devoid of the rich discussion and elaboration that can ensue.

Figure 30. Extended Anticipation Guide for Intermediate-Level Science Lesson on Sharks With Before-Reading Responses

Sharks!

Directions: Take turns reading each statement with your partners. Before reading the text, decide if you agree or disagree with the statement. Circle the upright shark fin if you agree and the upside-down shark fin if you disagree. Then, read *Sharks* by Carol Baldwin with your partner. After reading, decide if you agree or disagree with the statement. Then, write a brief statement justifying your response.

Agree	Disagree	Statement	Agree	Disagree	Justify
(fin)	fin	1. Sharks are warm-blooded mammals.	fin	fin	I heard on a TV program that they are, but I am not sure.
fin	(fin)	2. About 400 different species of sharks are known.	fin	fin	That sounds like too many. I would guess about 200.
(fin)	fin	3. Sharks have a keen sense of smell.	fin	fin	They smell blood, so you never want to go in deep water with a cut or anything.
(fin)	fin	4. Sharks have 30 rows of teeth in each jaw.	fin	fin	I think this is true. They can pull a man's leg off.
fin	(fin)	5. The skin of a shark is rough.	fin	fin	It looks smooth from pictures. I think this is false.
fin	(fin)	6. Some sharks live in rivers.	fin	fin	No way they can live in rivers. It has to be sea water.
(fin)	fin	7. Sharks live in both warm and cool habitats.	fin	fin	I think this is true. They are off the coast of NC, I know for sure, and Florida.
fin	(fin)	8. Sharks do not migrate.	fin	fin	I thought all fish migrate.
(fin)	fin	9. Sharks hunt in groups.	fin	fin	Yes, from other stories we read, fish group together in schools.
(fin)	fin	10. Sharks normally attack people.	fin	fin	If you are bleeding or moving around a lot, they will attack.
fin	(fin)	11. All sharks lay eggs.	fin	fin	Sharks don't lay eggs.
(fin)	fin	12. Sharks are killed for body parts.	fin	fin	This could be true, which is sad.

(continued)

With your partner, research the following websites:

www.sosforkids.com/sharks.html

www.nwf.org/kidzone/kzPage.crm?siteId=3&departmentId=82&articleId=1075

www.kidzworld.com/article/4188-saving-sharks

Then, create a poster informing your peers of ways to save sharks and why it is important. Include facts that you learned from the websites and from *Sharks* by Carol Baldwin. Be prepared to present your poster to your classmates.

Created by preservice teachers Schuyler Quinley, Alicia Jones, Jessica Bridges, and Shannon Burpeau of the University of North Carolina at Charlotte, USA. Reprinted with permission.

It is also important to establish a relaxed and comfortable environment in which students are free to risk their own opinions. Many students are unaccustomed to responding to open-ended statements; they are more familiar with questions for which there is a single correct answer. With this activity, they should be encouraged to make educated guesses based on their prior knowledge. For example, student exchange after reading the first statement in Part 1 of Figure 31 ("The Chinese government supports the right to freedom of speech.") might sound like the following:

Student A: Yeah, I think that's probably right. Everybody can say what they want here.

Student B: I don't know. I mean I know Americans can, but isn't China Communist?

Student C: Wait, I thought Communist had something to do with the economy, not free speech.

Student B: Well, I think it is both. Either way the government doesn't like anybody to disagree, at least that's what they were saying on the news last night.

In this case, the students are using their prior knowledge to engage in discussion. Students should always feel free to disagree with their partners. It is through shared experience that students' views of the world become broadened.

The extended writing portion is also most useful if done in pairs or small groups. Students then have the chance to share what they recall about the selection. After visiting the various websites about the Tiananmen Square protests, for instance, students would have discovered that they can use their prior knowledge to make connections to their learning as Student B shared. With the statements as their guides, they have the opportunity to make these discoveries on their own, as active readers.

Part 1: Read each statement and decide if you agree or disagree with it. Circle the character from the left-hand set that matches your views.

Decide		Statement	Reevaluate		Support Your View
Agree	Disagree		Agree	Disagree	
🙂	🙁	1. The Chinese government supports the right to freedom of speech.	🙂	🙁	Part 1: Agree Part 2: Disagree The government in China is Communist, and when the students were just having a peaceful protest the government came in and killed them.
🙂	🙁	2. The Tiananmen Square protests were violent demonstrations by angry students.	🙂	🙁	Part 1: Disagree Part 2: Disagree No, the students were just camping in the square and peacefully presenting some requests.
🙂	🙁	3. This demonstration has had a global impact on civil rights.	🙂	🙁	Part 1: Disagree Part 2: Agree People all over the world now know more about how China deals with protests, and it has made interest in civil rights grow.
🙂	🙁	4. Chinese people know about and are disgusted by the events in Tiananmen Square.	🙂	🙁	Part 1: Agree Part 2: Disagree The people of China do not know the full story of what happened because their government keeps information about this under wraps.
🙂	🙁	5. The total number of dead and injured was insignificant or unimportant.	🙂	🙁	Part 1: Disagree Part 2: Disagree The government made it sound like only a few people were killed, but it was for sure several hundred and some think it was more like a few thousand.

Part 2: Visit each of the sites listed below and gather information through what you see, hear, and read about the protests in Tiananmen Square, Peking (China), on June 4, 1989.

1. www.gwu.edu/~nsarchiv/NSAEBB/NSAEBB16/documents/index.html
   (Declassified documents collection from George Washington University)

2. www.thebeijingguide.com/tiananmen_square/index.html
   (360 degree virtual tour of Tiananmen Square)

3. news.bbc.co.uk/onthisday/hi/dates/stories/june/4/newsid_2496000/2496277.stm
   (BBC article from June 4, 1989)

4. video.google.com/videoplay?docid=1761062858590826090
   (Video footage of the protests from China)

5. www.breitbart.com/news/2006/01/24/D8FBCF686.html
   (Associated Press article on new Google China site)

6. en.wikipedia.org/wiki/Tiananmen_Square_protests_of_1989
   (Wikipedia, good background information)

Part 3: Consider the information you have collected from the websites. Reevaluate the statements and then support your final conclusions with evidence from the website resources.

Created by graduate student Aimee Grace Alder of the University of North Carolina at Charlotte, USA. Reprinted with permission.

Tips for Diverse Learners

- Use visual symbols and word-choice aids in making a speech-to-print match.
- Use websites, pictures, maps, or video clips.
- Display similar information in a variety of formats to allow students to have extended exposure to key concepts.

REFERENCES

Duffelmeyer, F.A., & Baum, D.D. (1992). The extended anticipation guide revisited. *Journal of Reading, 35,* 654–656.

Duffelmeyer, F.A., Baum, D.D., & Merkley, D.J. (1987). Maximizing reader-text confrontation with an extended anticipation guide. *Journal of Reading, 31,* 146–150.

Merkley, D.J. (1996–1997). Modified anticipation guide. *The Reading Teacher, 50,* 365–368.

Readence, J.E., Bean, T.W., & Baldwin, R.S. (1981). *Content area reading: An integrated approach.* Dubuque, IA: Kendall/Hunt.

Wood, K.D. (2000). *Literacy strategies across the subject areas: Process-oriented blackline masters for the K–12 classroom.* Boston: Allyn & Bacon.

Wood, K.D., & Harmon, J.M. (2001). *Strategies for integrating reading and writing in the middle and high school classroom.* Westerville, OH: National Middle School Association.

LITERATURE CITED

Baldwin, C. (2003). *Sharks.* Portsmouth, NH: Heinemann.

CHAPTER 13

Reaction Review Guide

Asking students to respond to a series of statements need not be restricted to science, social studies, and literature classes but can be applied to mathematics as well. For math in particular, we recommend using Reaction Review Guides because learning math involves the introduction of new concepts for which students often have insufficient prior knowledge. Consequently, we call this guide the Reaction Review Guide because students respond and "react" to the statements after reading and learning about new concepts as a means of solidifying their understanding of the information. Such a guide, used in the postreading stage of an instructional lesson only, is well suited to math lessons but can also be used in any subject where the teacher feels students may not have sufficient prior knowledge and experience to engage in a meaningful prereading discussion. We use math as an example in this chapter because brand new concepts are often presented sequentially, with which many students have had little or no experience. A student who had never had any experience calculating percentages, for example, would have difficulty discussing a statement such as, "Percent means every one hundred or out of one hundred." However, encountering the same statement *after* teacher explanation, group practice, and individual practice can aid students in thinking back over previous lessons and articulating their reactions and responses in the space provided on the guide.

Teachers often comment about the difficulty they have in getting students to refer back to their mathematics textbooks, in particular, to answer questions they may have and to refresh their memories about how to engage in a particular computation. They also sometimes have difficulty getting students to seek out assistance from other sources they may have provided in class including websites such as www.helpingwithmath.com, www.edhelper.com/math.htm, and www.algebrahelp.com. These sources often have ample examples and illustrations, so the Reaction Review Guide can help students use the textbook and other sources approved by the

Grade Levels
Primary, intermediate, middle, secondary

Subjects
Math, content areas

Classroom Contexts
Pairs, small groups, whole class

Guiding Readers Through Text: Strategy Guides for New Times (2nd ed.) by Karen D. Wood, Diane Lapp, James Flood, and D. Bruce Taylor. © 2008 by the International Reading Association.

teacher as resources. In addition, while the primary way writing is integrated through mathematics is often through word problems, the Reaction Review Guide provides another vehicle for integrating writing across the math curriculum.

When designing the guide, we recommend that teachers include a combination of written statements reflecting the key concepts in the lesson as well as computational examples. We recommend that the teacher should reflect on the most significant content presented over the course of a lesson or unit and then develop somewhere between 5 and 10 statements worded as either true or false to encourage students to think before they answer. We suggest that students work in pairs for this activity with the directive to look back in their textbook, notes, online sources, or other sources to support their answers. As with any of the strategy guides in this book, teacher modeling of at least one example is conducive to fewer questions and improved responses from students. We have found that students perform much better on subsequent tests after including this review activity with a lesson. Again, while we illustrate the Reaction Review Guide with mathematics, it can be applied to any subject area where the teacher deems extra review may be needed to further student understanding.

In Figure 32, we show how the concept of using statements can be used after a lesson or unit to solidify students' understanding of important math concepts (see page 187 in the Appendix for a reproducible version of this guide). The guide shown in Figure 32 was used after intermediate-level students studied the concept of perimeter during their math period. Notice how the students referred back to their text to justify the answers to specific statements. The guide also provided students with the opportunity to reflect on how and why they would use a specific math concept in everyday life, as shown in statement number 5: "There are many situations in everyday life in which we would need to know how to find the perimeter."

As with many of the other guides in this text, we recommend that teachers allow students to work together to solve problems, discuss, and share their thinking. Then the teacher can listen in on the responses and help clarify misunderstandings before the unit test. The Reaction Review Guide becomes a vehicle for reviewing the key concepts of a lesson with group members under the aegis of the teacher.

Tips for Diverse Learners

- Pair second-language learners with English-speaking learners.
- Read the statements aloud beforehand and point to each word as you read.
- Provide additional whole-class or small-group instruction where needed on specific topics.

Figure 32. Reaction Review Guide for Intermediate-Level Math Lesson on Perimeter

Names of Group Members: Scott, Jordi

Topic: Measurement: Area & Perimeter

Directions: With your partner, take turns reading and discussing each of the statements below. Put a check if you agree or disagree with each statement. Be sure to support your answer with at least one example. Use your book or any other sources for support.

1. An example of when you may need to know the perimeter would be if you were building a pen for your dog.

    _____✓_____ I agree   _____ I disagree

    because: We built a pretend pen for our class dog.

2. To find the perimeter of an object you multiply all four sides.

    _____ I agree   _____✓_____ I disagree

    because: You add all sides not multiply them.

3. We would need to know the area of our classroom if we were going to carpet the room.

    _____✓_____ I agree   _____ I disagree

    because: You don't want to put carpet around the edges. Our glossary says area covers the total surface.

4. To find the area, you multiply all four sides together.

    _____ I agree   _____✓_____ I disagree

    because: We learned you have to multiply only two sides together, length X width.

5. There are many situations in everyday life in which we would need to know how to find the perimeter.

    _____✓_____ I agree   _____ I disagree

    because: When you build a house or a building, you need to use the area to see how much surface you cover.

From Wood, K.D., & Harmon, J.M. (2001). *Strategies for integrating reading and writing in the middle and high school classroom* (p. 109). Westerville, OH: National Middle School Association. Reprinted with the permission of the National Middle School Association.

REFERENCES

Wood, K.D., & Harmon, J.M. (2001). *Strategies for integrating reading and writing in the middle and high school classroom*. Westerville, OH: National Middle School Association.

PART V

Manipulative Guides

Manipulative Guides are three-dimensional tools for organizing information and helping students make sense of information across grade levels and subject areas. Manipulative Guides work much like graphic organizers but are more interactive and fun to create. Guides such as the Foldable Guide not only allow students to organize information but also create a valuable study tool helping them review information for tests. As the name suggests, Manipulative Guides are a fun, hands-on way to help students with comprehension, vocabulary, and learning.

CHAPTER 14

Foldable Guide

According to Zike (2002), a "foldable" is "a 3-D, student-made, interactive graphic organizer based upon a skill" (p. 1). There is little research that focuses on foldables in reading and learning, as foldables receive little attention in journals and teacher education books; however, like Zike, we see Foldable Guides as graphic organizers, and graphic organizers of all types, of course, are ubiquitous in content area literacy books (Readence, Bean, & Baldwin, 2004; Vacca & Vacca, 2004). Like traditional graphic organizers, foldables come in many forms and are limited only by imagination. Foldable Guides are an engaging way to help students learn content-specific vocabulary in various subject areas, or, as in one of our examples, to help ELLs with English vocabulary.

Foldable Guides offer many instructional possibilities. Students can work in small groups, pairs, or individually to create Foldable Guides. Moreover, Foldable Guides work in any subject area and can be paired with other activities. For instance, Foldable Guides can be a great project for literature circle groups or for learning vocabulary specific to a unit of study in science or math.

While it is not the scope of this book to explore foldables in depth, in this chapter we share ideas that teachers with whom we have collaborated have found useful.

Grade Levels
Intermediate, middle, secondary

Subjects
Reading/language arts, social studies, science, fine arts

Classroom Contexts
Individuals, small groups, whole class, tutoring sessions

Flip Charts

Flip charts are a simple but powerful way for students to organize information about a unit of study. By stacking four to five sheets of 8½" by 11" paper at even intervals of about ½ inch apart, students can then fold over these sheets to create a flip chart (see page 188 in the Appendix for a reproducible version of these instructions).

One teacher used flip charts with her fourth-grade students after reading the book *Auntie Claus* by Elise Primavera (1999) in which the students created a plot map of the book listing the main events (see Figure 33). One student wrote, "Sophie stowed away to find out what Auntie Claus does on her business trip" on the first page and then on the second, "Sophie arrived at the North Pole and looked like an elf. She volunteered to go set the BB&G list. When she found the list, her brother's name was on it. She erased it and replaced it with hers." Students illustrated the flip charts with drawings to represent key plot elements.

Cindy Hovis, a K–3 teacher of ELLs, uses flip charts to help her students learn writing conventions (such as capitalization and key vocabulary concepts). Figure 34 is an example of a flip chart she used with early elementary–level ELL students to provide them with specific examples of when to capitalize words in English. This teacher-created flip chart titled "Flipping Over Capitalization" includes the following categories:

Figure 33. Plot Map Flip Chart for Primavera's *Auntie Claus*

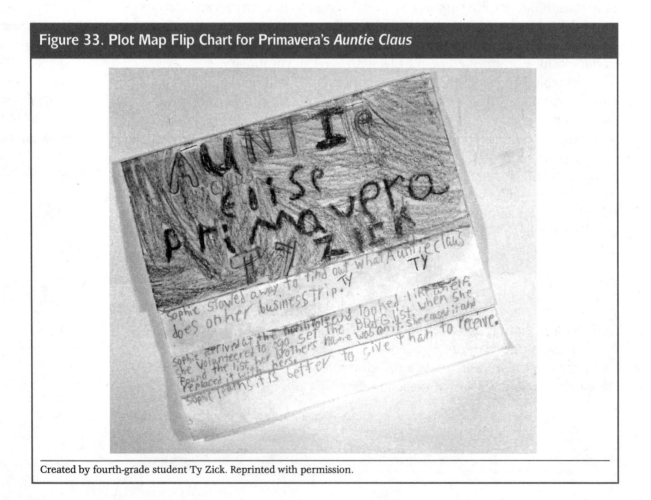

Created by fourth-grade student Ty Zick. Reprinted with permission.

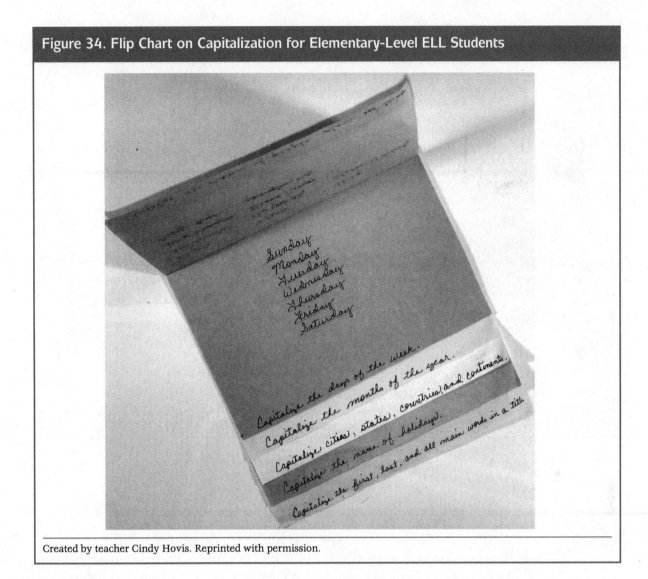

Sunday
Monday
Tuesday
Wednesday
Thursday
Friday
Saturday

Capitalize the days of the week.

Capitalize the months of the year.

Capitalize cities, states, countries, and continents.

Capitalize the name of holidays.

Capitalize the first, last, and all main words in a title.

Created by teacher Cindy Hovis. Reprinted with permission.

- Capitalize the pronoun *I*
- Capitalize the first word in a sentence
- Capitalize the names of people, places, and things
- Capitalize the days of the week
- Capitalize the months of the year
- Capitalize cities, states, countries, and continents
- Capitalize the names of holidays
- Capitalize the first, last, and all main words in a title

As can be seen in Figure 34, the teacher included examples under each category.

Figure 35. Tabbed Book on Farm Life for Elementary-Level ELL Students

Created by teacher Cindy Hovis. Reprinted with permission.

Tabbed Books

A tabbed book is another type of Foldable Guide similar to a flip chart. Tabbed books are easy to make: 8½" by 11" paper is folded in half lengthwise and stapled together to form a book. Then, overlapping pieces are cut from each page beginning at the front of the book so that a tab is left on each page.

Figure 35 is an example used by the same ELL teacher who created the Foldable Guide in Figure 34. Because many of her students lived in a rural area, the teacher had students create a tabbed book titled "My Farm Book." This example integrates more visual elements than the flip chart on capitalization, which is an excellent way to make vocabulary and concept learning more effective.

Flap Books and Tri-Folds

It would be easy to think of Foldable Guides as working primarily in the elementary grades, but as we will see they can be used effectively in middle and high school classrooms. A colleague of ours who teaches high school history uses flap books and tri-folds to help her students organize and learn content relating to units in her U.S. history course. For example, Figure 36 is an example of a flap book she has students create on the topic of the U.S. Civil War. Her instructions were as follows: "Create a foldable timeline that includes the following items: Compromise of 1850, Fugitive Slave Act/Personal Liberty Laws, Underground Railroad, Uncle Tom's Cabin, Kansas–Nebraska Act, Bleeding Kansas, Lincoln–Douglas Debates, and Harper's Ferry." Students used multiple sources, including their textbooks, library books, and information gleaned from the Internet, to research these topics and create their flap books.

Construction of the flap book is simple. The teacher provided students with construction paper, scissors, and glue sticks. Students folded a piece of construction paper in half to create a book and then cut out and glued smaller folded geometric shapes (circular pieces in the flap book found in Figure 36) on the cover and insides of their flap book. Students wrote the topic, such as "The Compromise of 1850," on the

Figure 36. "Road to Civil War" Flap Book for Secondary-Level Students

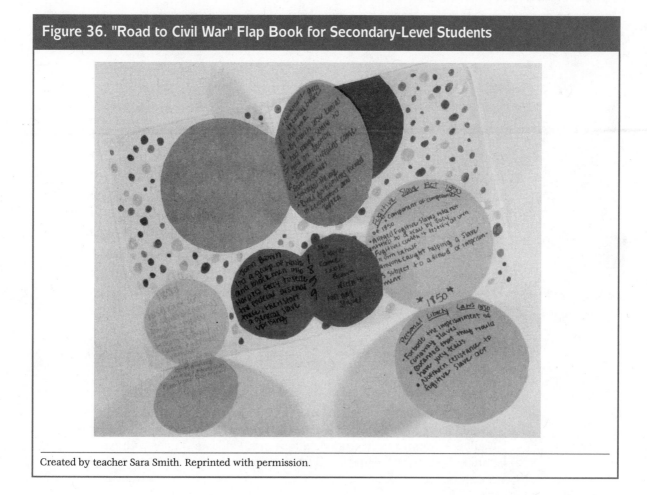

Created by teacher Sara Smith. Reprinted with permission.

Figure 37. Tri-fold for Unit on New Deal Programs

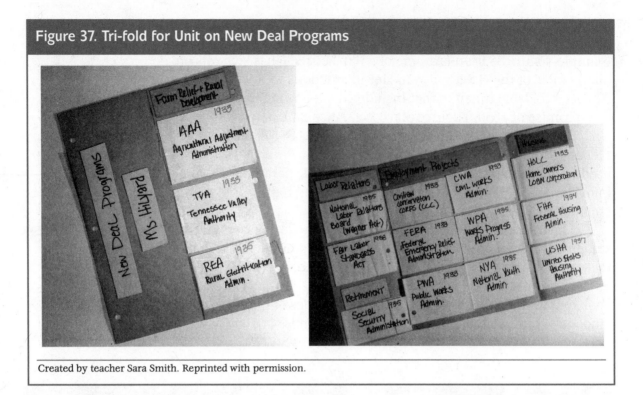

Created by teacher Sara Smith. Reprinted with permission.

cover of a flap and wrote a summary of what they had learned on the inside of the flap.

Tri-folds are another creative way for students to synthesize what they learn. Simply put, a tri-fold is a piece of paper folded into thirds so that it creates panels or columns not unlike a two- or three-column journal. These can be either very simple or more elaborate. Figure 37 illustrates a tri-fold on the New Deal programs created for a high school history class. The tri-folds served as a study tool and helped students keep track of different New Deal programs they were learning about in class. This activity could be paired with another strategy guide, such as the Inquiry Guide (see chapter 7), to help students organize information before constructing their tri-folds or flap books.

Tips for Diverse Learners

- In order not to overwhelm ELL students, focus on fewer elements and concepts.
- Pair ELL students with other students—if possible, with multilingual students who have competency in English and their partners' primary language.
- Allow students to construct dual-language Foldable Guides with parts that are in their primary language and parts in English.

REFERENCES

Readence, J.E., Bean, T.W., & Baldwin, R.S. (2004). *Content area literacy: An integrated approach* (8th ed.). Dubuque, IA: Kendall/Hunt.

Vacca, R.T., & Vacca, J.A.L. (2004). *Content area reading: Literacy and learning across the curriculum* (8th ed.). Boston: Allyn & Bacon.

Zike, D. (2002). *Dinah Zike's reading and study skills foldables*. New York: McGraw Hill.

LITERATURE CITED

Primavera, E. (1999). *Auntie Claus*. New York: Silver Whistle.

CHAPTER 15

Origami Guide

L ike the Foldable Guides in chapter 14, the Origami Guide is a three-dimensional format for collecting and organizing information and, like other Foldable Guides, it functions much like a graphic organizer. The Origami Guide can be used to organize information in any subject area. For example, an English language arts teacher could have students create a story map, plot outline, or character map with an Origami Guide. Students in an earth science class could organize types of rocks or minerals using the Origami Guide, while in a geometry course students could organize theorems or formulas associated with geometric shapes, such as area and volume. What distinguishes the Origami Guide from other types of Foldable Guides is its compact format and engaging appeal for students. Origami Guides are fun to make.

The instructions and recommendations for creating and using Origami Guides are outlined in the following sections.

Grade Levels
Intermediate, middle, secondary

Subjects
Reading/language arts, social studies, science, fine arts

Classroom Contexts
Individuals, small groups

Step 1: Acquiring the Materials

The following materials are necessary in order to make the Origami Guide:

- four to six sheets of paper cut to a square ($8\frac{1}{2}$" by $8\frac{1}{2}$") per student
- two square pieces of cardboard per student ($4\frac{1}{2}$" by $4\frac{1}{2}$")
- glue sticks
- scissors

We recommend that teachers have these materials assembled and organized ahead of time.

Guiding Readers Through Text: Strategy Guides for New Times (2nd ed.) by Karen D. Wood, Diane Lapp, James Flood, and D. Bruce Taylor. © 2008 by the International Reading Association.

Step 2: Assembling the "Guts"

Demonstrate to the class how to assemble the Origami Guide by modeling it for the class. Begin by creating the "guts" of the Origami Guide by taking one sheet of the 8½" by 8½" paper and folding it diagonally through the center. Unfold this and then fold the paper in half first horizontally and then vertically. Be sure all folds are crisp; it helps to press each fold with scissors or a ruler. (For a visual explanation of how to fold the paper and assemble the "guts," see page 189 in the Appendix for a reproducible version of these instructions.)

The number of sheets of paper used determines the length, but four to seven pieces of paper works well. Fold each piece of paper the same way and glue them together "tip to tail" as shown in the Appendix. After the pieces are glued together, students can complete the guts of the Origami Guide by folding each section into a 4¼" square by pinching the corners of the diagonal fold together, as illustrated in Figure 38.

Figure 38. Illustration of the Final Folds of an Origami Guide

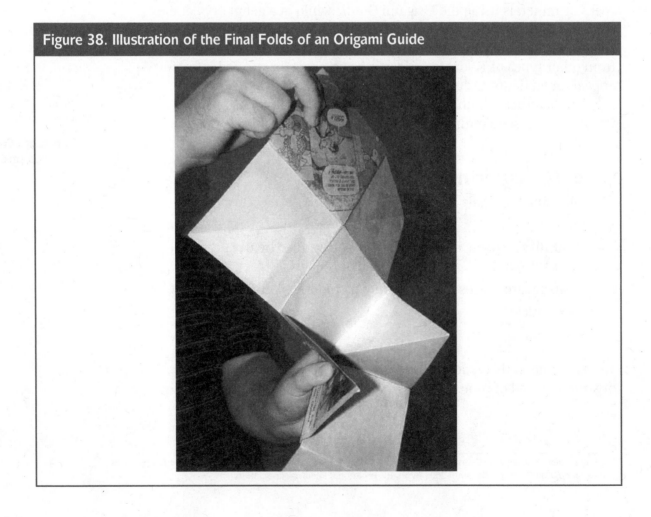

Origami Guide

Figure 39. Completed Origami Guide

Step 3: Making the Covers

Once the guts are assembled, students can create covers for both sides of the Origami Guide by taking the two squares of cardboard—which are cut just slightly larger than the folded guts—and covering them with newsprint, wrapping paper, or fabric. Cut the cover material to about 5½" square and have students center the cardboard on the cover material. Glue the cover to the cardboard, wrapping the cardboard. Glue the covers to the ends of the folded guts with the fully covered sides of the cardboard to the outside. Figure 39 shows an example of a completed Origami Guide.

Step 4: Uses for the Origami Guide

Uses for the Origami Guide are limited only by the imagination of teachers and students. Origami Guides can be used in many ways in English language arts. They can be used for multigenre narratives but also can be used as story maps for a novel or as a character journal in which students write entries from the point of view of a character in a novel or story. They can be used in literature circles as an alternative to a book report or to keep track of literary terms. In Figure 40 an Origami

Figure 40. Reading Biography Origami Guide

Guide was used to illustrate a reading autobiography featuring the names of books and key events in the reader's development. Figure 41 provides an example of a guide created by a high school student in her English class of her literary autobiography or timeline; she wrote this about her literate life: "Recently, I enjoy reading mysteries, comedies, and books a little out of the ordinary, such as *The Executioner's Daughter* (Williams, 2000), *Despereaux* (DiCamillo, 2003), and the *House of the Scorpion*

Figure 41. Secondary Student's Literary Timeline

(Farmer, 2002)." Both examples show how visual and textual elements can be combined for a creative approach to organizing and documenting information.

While the sample Origami Guides in Figures 40 and 41 are examples from the English language arts content area, Origami Guides can be adapted to any content area. The following are a few examples of how they can be used across subject areas.

Math

Students use the Origami Guide to outline important math concepts and formulas. For instance, students in a geometry class could list formulas for the area and volume of geometric shapes such as cylinders, cubes, and spheres alongside drawings of each shape. These math guides are excellent tools to help students in studying.

Science

Students can work in teams to gather information on a topic with each team creating an Origami Guide to represent what they learned. For example, students in a biology class could work in groups to study different systems in the human body such as the circulatory system, nervous system, and different sensory functions such as sight and hearing.

History

The structure of the Origami Guide lends itself quite well to the creation of a timeline or historical report. Students studying World War II could create a visual timeline of the war as they read the text and progress through the unit. They could include key events with visual images. As with the math example above, this timeline would be a good tool to help students study for a test.

Art

In an art class, the Origami Guide is a terrific way to integrate artistic effects with inquiry and study about an artist or period of art. Students can also use them to represent what they learn about a specific genre or medium of art.

Tips for Diverse Learners

- Pair ELL students with other students—if possible with multilingual students who have competency in English and their partners' primary language.
- Limit the scope of inquiry so that ELL students can focus on learning a manageable amount of content. Stress depth over breadth of knowledge.
- Origami Guides are an excellent format for a dual-language vocabulary journal or personal dictionary. Students can write words in their primary language as well as English and add a visual element such as a picture to help with vocabulary growth.

LITERATURE CITED

DiCamillo, K. (2003). *The tale of Despereaux: Being the story of a mouse, a princess, some soup, and a spool of thread.* Cambridge, MA: Candlewick.

Farmer, N. (2002). *The house of the scorpion.* New York: Atheneum.

Williams, L.E. (2000). *The executioner's daughter.* New York: Henry Holt.

PART VI

Text Structure Guides

Students who have an understanding of how various text formats are structured have fewer problems with comprehension. The guides in this section help students develop an awareness that not all texts are structured in the same way and that understanding the way authors present information can aid their own comprehension. As such, these guides help students organize their thinking to coordinate with the varied text structures they will encounter while reading from multiple text sources.

CHAPTER 16

Analogical Strategy Guide

The notion of making content area information, such as science, more accessible and comprehendible through literacy strategies is supported by Spencer and Guillaume (2006). They suggest using prevalent practices in literacy instruction while teaching new vocabulary in content areas. Often, teachers rely on the textbook and textbook practices to teach new vocabulary. However, vocabulary found in science books probably will not appear in math books, or social studies books, and so on; therefore, it is necessary for students to understand these new words outside of the context.

One way to do this is to extend the vocabulary usage beyond the context in which it appears through the use of analogy. When new information is presented through the use of analogies, it often becomes more vivid and easily understood by students because of their familiarity with the initial concept. Bean, Singer, and Cowan (1985) used this notion to develop the Analogical Strategy Guide, which supports the learning of content information by making abstract concepts more imaginable and by encouraging students to connect new information with everyday experiences. Therefore, the Analogical Strategy Guide will be beneficial in what Spencer and Guillaume (2006) call the "engage and explore" phases of content vocabulary development, which can be a part of learning from any type of text.

There are three steps recommended by Bean and colleagues (1985) in developing an Analogical Strategy Guide. The first step is to analyze the reading task to determine what concepts students will be expected to learn. Focus only on essential information and eliminate the rest from

Grade Levels
Primary, intermediate, middle, secondary

Subjects
Any content area

Classroom Contexts
Individuals, small groups, whole class

Guiding Readers Through Text: Strategy Guides for New Times (2nd ed.) by Karen D. Wood, Diane Lapp, James Flood, and D. Bruce Taylor. © 2008 by the International Reading Association.

further study; doing this will reinforce the notion for students that textbooks are a reference source from which the most important information can be gleaned.

The second step is to construct appropriate analogies. Many content area topics, especially those that introduce many new vocabulary terms, lend themselves well to comparisons with things familiar to students (although Bean et al. also caution that it is not always possible to develop analogies for the concept of study). For an example of a content area topic that lends itself well to analogy, see the Analogical Strategy Guide in Figure 42, which makes the science topic of the circulatory system easier for students to understand by comparing each function to an element of road systems (see page 190 in the Appendix for a reproducible version of this guide). This Analogical Strategy Guide was inspired by Bean et al.'s (1985) analogical cell model in which they use analogy to demonstrate how the 14 parts of a cell function similarly to the various parts of a factory.

For example, the cell wall, whose main function is to provide support and protection, is related to factory walls. The cell membrane, which forms a boundary and serves as gatekeeper, is compared to the factory security guards. The cell nucleus, which contains the organism's genetic coding, is analogous to the boss's office with a copy machine. In Figure 42, instead of comparing the 14 functions of a cell to the various parts of a factory, this intermediate-level science lesson uses analogies to describe the circulatory system. To further enhance this step, if a diagram for the concept being taught is included in the lesson, students could draw analogies/comparisons onto the diagram.

The third crucial step in this process is to explain and demonstrate to students how the guide works. Illustrating how analogies can be used as retrieval cues or mnemonic devices to help students recall information learned from text is important. Students can be encouraged to develop their own analogies about a given topic to further enhance their learning. We believe such a task could best be accomplished in small, heterogeneous groups where students can brainstorm and try out their ideas with their peers.

While making analogies, it is also important for teachers to clarify both the content vocabulary word being taught as well as the term to which it is being compared. For example, in Figure 42 hemoglobin is being compared to gasoline; this analogy will be irrelevant if students have no background knowledge of gasoline or its use. For this purpose, we have included pictures in the Analogical Strategy Guide. The pictures can act as a reference guide as well as activating prior knowledge to make the analogies more meaningful; if a student does not recall the word *gasoline* but does recognize the picture, thus activating prior knowledge, then the analogy to hemoglobin will be better understood.

Figure 42. Analogical Strategy Guide for Intermediate-Level Science Lesson on the Circulatory System

Element of Circulatory System	Picture	Function	Similar Element of Road System	Picture
Red Blood Cells	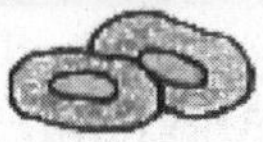	Carry gases to and from the body's cells	Cars	
Hemoglobin		Protein that carries oxygen to the body	Gasoline	
Bone Marrow	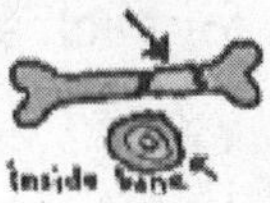	Makes red blood cells	Car factories and dealers	
White Blood Cells		Fight diseases and infections	Traffic cop	
Platelets		Produce blood clots that stop the bleeding	Construction barrier	
Arteries	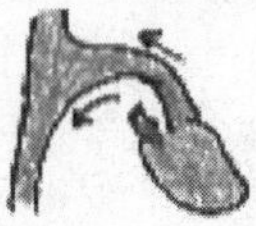	Carry blood away from the heart	Highways	
Veins	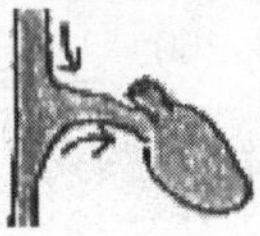	Carry blood to the heart	Numbered routes (more rural than highway)	
Capillaries	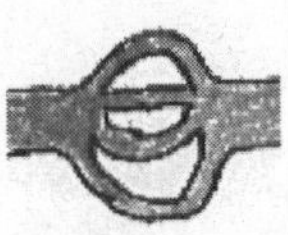	Connect arteries to veins	Exit ramp off freeway	
Heart	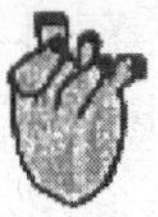	Muscular organ that pumps blood to the body	City	

The Analogical Strategy Guide can be taken to the next level by removing sections, such as providing information in all columns but the "Function" column or the comparison column ("Similar Elements"). Thus, from the vocabulary words and analogies alone, students will have to describe the function. This can be taken yet another step further by removing all text and only leaving the pictures. When the pictures are scrambled, students will have to match the "Element of the Circulatory System" to its appropriate "Similar Element of the Road System."

In Figure 43, using ideas presented in Spencer and Guillaume's (2006) article, we followed their suggested method of teaching vocabulary with the use of Analogical Strategy Guides through engaging the student in learning, exploring what is to be learned, developing a plan for learning, and applying the plan (see page 191 in the Appendix for a reproducible version of this guide). Here a middle-level social studies lesson on early inhabitants of California and sample student responses are shown; students will follow the directions for each section of the strategy guide to create their own analogies.

Tips for Diverse Learners

- Frontload vocabulary and use pictures with a word bank if possible.
- Be sure to discuss and describe what is being discussed in the analogy (e.g., in Bean et al.'s [1985] cell analogy to a factory, make sure students know what a factory is and the different parts of it).
- For concrete items, bring in realia (pictures of a factory) so students visually see the comparison.

REFERENCES

Bean, T.W., Singer, H., & Cowan, S. (1985). Analogical study guides: Improving comprehension in science. *Journal of Reading, 29,* 246–250.

Spencer, B.H., & Guillaume, A.M. (2006). Integrating curriculum through the learning cycle: Content-based reading and vocabulary instruction. *The Reading Teacher, 60,* 206–219.

Follow the directions for each section.

1. **Engage.** In the following box, list all the words or ideas you think of when you hear "Early People in California." (You have three minutes to do this.)

> **Early People in California**
>
> Covered wagons
> People crossing the land bridge in Alaska
> Gold
> Spanish and Mexicans
> Zorro
> Not a lot of women
> Indians

2. **Explore.** With a partner, read each of the following vocabulary words. Go back to the text and find where the word is used; use context clues to decipher what each word means. In the box below write your working definition next to each word.

Vocabulary Word	Your Definition
Fort (p. 45)	A place where the soldiers are stationed and you can be safe
Presidio (p. 50)	A kind of fort on the water to protect from pirates
Pueblo (p. 51)	The villages of the first people living in California
Rancho (p. 51)	The Spanish word for ranch
Arrowhead (p. 54)	The sharp tip of an arrow that is made out of rock or metal
Long House (p. 55)	A long skinny house that the native people lived in
Canoe (p. 55)	A little boat made out of animal skins or a hollowed-out tree

(continued)

3. Develop. Using the definitions you created for the vocabulary words above, create an Analogical Strategy Guide. To do this, reflect on the definitions you created, then in the following chart, create an analogy for each word to something of today's people and draw an appropriate picture if possible.

Element of Early People in California Vocabulary Word	Picture	Function	Similar Element of Today's People	Picture
Fort		A home for the army and to protect the people	Army base	
Presidio		To protect against pirates	Coast Guard	
Pueblo		A home made of mud and clay	Root cellar	
Rancho		A place where cattle or other animals are raised	Ranch	
Arrowhead		Hunting or fighting	Bullet	
Long House		Communal living	Apartment building	
Canoe		Transportation	Car	

(continued)

4. Apply. Refer back to the Analogical Strategy Guide you made as well as the definitions for the vocabulary words you thought of with your partner. Applying the knowledge you have of these words, write a paragraph (narrative or expository) using at least four of the new vocabulary words correctly. The words should be used so that if a person who had no prior knowledge of the vocabulary were to read your paragraph he or she would be able to determine what the words meant by using the context clues you have given.

If you visit California you may find evidence of the people who lived there a long time ago. Sometimes pueblos and long houses are preserved by museums so that we can see how and where people used to live. There are old forts that you can visit too and lots of them have an armory where they keep all kinds of old weapons like arrowheads.

CHAPTER 17

Concept Guide

Grade Levels
Primary, intermediate,
middle, secondary

Subjects
Any content area

Classroom Contexts
Individuals, small groups,
whole class

Concept Guides, designed by Baker (1977), are intended to help students organize information from any selected print-based text by categorizing minor details or information under major concepts. Baker believes that within any pattern of organization, certain concepts are more important than others and that students need help in distinguishing the most significant concepts from the less significant. Therefore, the first part of a Concept Guide contains literal-level tasks and questions relating to the selected text. In the second part, students must place details or supporting ideas from the text under major concepts. An optional third section might involve a deeper level of generalization or inferencing in which students are required to find textual support for major concepts.

Because all students can benefit from assistance in organizing subordinate information under major concepts, the Concept Guide can be geared for students at any grade level. Figures 44 and 45 offer examples of developmentally appropriate content guides. The Concept Guide on animal migration for elementary students in Figure 44 was developed as a learning tool for individual students or small groups (see page 193 in the Appendix for a reproducible version of this guide). First, in Part 1 of the Concept Guide, students place statements directly under either "True" or "False" headings according to their prior knowledge. During this part of the activity, the teacher should instigate an in-depth class discussion. Although the statements themselves are at the literal level, the thinking that goes into determining placement requires higher levels of thought. Next, students are instructed to read/listen to the text while keeping the prior statements in mind. Last, the class will move on to Part 2 of the guide working as individuals or in small groups in order to go over their prereading choices and rearrange the statements to fall under the correct headings, being certain to use textual support for any

Guiding Readers Through Text: Strategy Guides for New Times (2nd ed.) by Karen D. Wood, Diane Lapp, James Flood, and D. Bruce Taylor. © 2008 by the International Reading Association.

changes made. Students can refer back to their rearranged concept list in Part 1 or to their text for assistance. The class as a whole may discuss the categorized terms to complete the activity. Because younger students often enjoy hands-on learning activities, an adaptation of the printed version of this guide would be to hand out teacher-created sentence strips and word cards for the students to complete as partners to be put together like a puzzle.

In another example, Figure 45 shows a Concept Guide for a middle-level history lesson on the U.S. Civil War (see page 194 in the Appendix for a reproducible version of this guide). Part 1 of the guide asks students to take note of the most important concepts and ideas in a text through the incorporation of a style of note-taking inspired by Cornell Notes, introduced by Walter Pauk in the 1950s (see Pauk, 2000). To engage in taking Cornell Notes, the paper needs to be divided into two columns. The column on the right is usually where the notes are written by the student. As illustrated in Figure 45, the note-taking column should be larger than the column on the left, where the keywords or questions are later written by the student. While listening to a lecture, watching a video, or reading any assigned text, notes are taken in the "Note-Taking Column." After the reading or listening is completed, the student reviews the notes and writes keywords or questions in the "Cue Column." After reviewing the keywords, the student then uses the last four lines to write a short summary. Students should regularly cover up the note-taking column and review the questions and keywords in the Cue Column, as this practice instantiates the information in the student's mind. Cornell note-taking is very popular because of the degree of student engagement that is required. In Part 2 of the guide, which is similar to the literal-level task seen in the Learning-From-Text Guide (see page 65 in chapter 8), students are instructed to read the selected text on their own and then work in groups to determine which statements can be supported by the text they read. An ending activity for this lesson is the construction of a timeline in Part 3, which further encourages students to use details from the text to form generalizations; this activity forces students to categorize information about the war from the most important to the least since there were many smaller, less significant battles fought.

Tips for Diverse Learners

- Pair ELL students with English-speaking students to ensure that comprehension will occur.
- Frontload vocabulary before activity.
- When able, incorporate pictures with vocabulary words and use a word bank.

Part 1. Directions: Place each of these statements under either the "true" or the "false" heading.

True

In autumn, many animals stay where they are for winter.
When animals migrate, they move from one home to another.
During autumn, weather is warmer in the south.
Animals usually migrate by themselves.
A flock is a group of geese.
Whales do not eat during autumn or winter.

False

True

When animals migrate, they move from one home to another.
During autumn, weather is warmer in the south.
A flock is a group of geese.
Whales do not eat during autumn or winter.

False

In autumn, many animals stay where they are for winter.
Animals usually migrate by themselves.

Part 2. Directions: From the information given in the text, complete a closed sort by placing each word or phrase from the word bank under the correct heading. (Examples below illustrate how this can be done.)

Headings

Migrate   Emigrate   Reasons Animals Migrate   Groups of Animals

Word Bank

Flock   Weather   To move from one home to another   Pod

To move from one country to another country to live   Water in the north freezes

Herd   Plants die   Moving in a V-shape   Animals move together in a group

Migrate
Moving in a V-shape
To move from one home to another
Animals move together in a group

Emigrate
To move from one country to another country to live

Reasons Animals Migrate
Water in the north freezes
Plants die
Weather

Groups of Animals
Herd
Flock
Pod

Figure 45. Concept Guide for Middle-Level History Lesson on the U.S. Civil War

Topic: Civil War

Part 1. Directions: On your own, complete the following Cornell Notes–inspired strategy guide as you read. Remember what we have learned about Cornell Notes as you fill in the chart and also that we are working to recognize and categorize main ideas from the supporting details. You can always incorporate supporting details in the summary section of the guide, because it may not be necessary to include these in the main portion. When you are done with your reading and have completed the Cornell Notes, meet with your group and compare notes; if you are missing any important details or have any new questions, add them to your guide.

Cue Column:	Note-Taking Column:
Who was involved?	US states union and confederacy
When?	1861-1865
Union	23 northern states
Confederacy	11 southern states
Why were they fighting	Confederacy wanted to secede from union
Major Issue	Slavery
Results	13th amendment-abolished slavery

Summary:

The civil war of the United States was based on the fact that 11 southern states wanted the right to continue to own their slaves and the northern states believed everyone should be free.

Part 2. Directions: Read the selected portion of the text from *A Nation Torn: The Story of How the Civil War Began* on your own. Then, in groups, discuss each printed statement below and place a checkmark next to the ones that are specifically supported by the text you just read.

_____1. In the 1800s people were brought from Africa to the United States and sold to white landowners.

_____2. A regiment is a group of soldiers.

_____3. Many types of weapons were used during the U.S. Civil War. Instead of rifles or muskets, soldiers used machine guns.

_____4. The North produced three-fourths of the nation's wealth, their army was bigger, and thousands of black soldiers fought with their army.

_____5. The North had better generals than the South, like Robert E. Lee and Thomas "Stonewall" Jackson.

(continued)

____6. In 1863, President Lincoln put the Emancipation Proclamation to work. He declared the slaves in all Confederate areas to be "forever free."

____7. Southerners supported President Lincoln and wanted to be part of the Union.

____8. Jefferson Davis was the President of the Confederate States of America as well as the commander in chief of the Confederate army.

Part 3. Directions: Working with your group, use the information in Parts 1 and 2 to create a timeline that highlights major dates during the U.S. Civil War. Your timeline should include beginning and ending dates of the war as well as the dates of significant battles and new laws instilled in the government. Use the years printed as guidelines for plotting only the most important dates. When complete, you should have at least 10 of the most important dates or events included on your timeline.

1861	1862	1863	1864	1865

REFERENCES

Baker, R.L. (1977). The effects of informational organizers on learning and retention, content knowledge, and term relationships in ninth grade social studies. In H.L. Herber & R.T. Vacca (Eds.), *Research in reading in the content areas: The third report* (pp. 134–150). Syracuse, NY: Syracuse University Reading and Language Arts Center.

Pauk, W. (2000). *How to study in college* (7th ed.). Boston: Houghton Mifflin

CHAPTER 18

Pattern Guide

According to Vacca and Vacca (2002), it is crucial for readers to use and identify text patterns while reading in order to thoroughly comprehend text, as text patterns offer the reader cues about how the information is organized. Incorporating a Pattern Guide is a great way for teachers to assist students to recognize patterns and relationships in texts of many formats. Understanding the organizational pattern facilitates learning within and across categories. Herber (1970) and Vacca (1981) say the primary purpose of the Pattern Guide is to help students become responsive to the various ways textbook selections can be organized (e.g., cause and effect, compare and contrast, sequence, enumeration). This type of strategy guide is developed to coordinate with the predominant pattern of a given text. The underlying assumption of the Pattern Guide is that the ability to recognize text organization is a highly sophisticated skill that most readers do not develop independently. A Pattern Guide scrambles the text's organization and requires students to piece it back together in a logical order. Students must examine and think about the relationships that exist within the given pattern in order to do this.

A number of forms can be taken when creating a Pattern Guide; the form depends on the subject as well as the learning level of the students. While the form may differ, the basic procedure for using Pattern Guides remains the same. The following is a modified version of the teaching sequence recommended by Herber (1970), Vacca (1981), and Vacca and Vacca (2002).

Step 1. Before implementing the Pattern Guide, examine the text selection to determine the most prevalent pattern. Keep in mind that patterns of text can vary throughout a book and that students are frequently unable to determine these patterns without sufficient teacher guidance.

Grade Levels
Primary, intermediate, middle, secondary

Subjects
Reading/language arts, social studies, science, fine arts

Classroom Contexts
Individuals, small groups, whole class

Guiding Readers Through Text: Strategy Guides for New Times (2nd ed.) by Karen D. Wood, Diane Lapp, James Flood, and D. Bruce Taylor. © 2008 by the International Reading Association.

Step 2. Advise students on the pattern of the text; explain to students that their content area books contain various text patterns and that recognizing and using these patterns can further their understanding of the material.

Step 3. Model and guide students when introducing a text format or if they are having difficulty. In whole or small groups, discuss the text pattern under study by using everyday examples before asking students to transfer their knowledge to their reading assignment. For example, if you are discussing the compare-and-contrast pattern, you might want to draw students' attention to words that signal this pattern (see Table 2). Next, model how these signal words are used in everyday speaking and reading to indicate that items, events, or people are being compared and/or contrasted. Consider the following example: "Deserts may look desolate, but they are home to many species."

Step 4. Assist students, and be certain that whole-class and small-group discussions are used frequently throughout the lesson to further solidify understanding and to correct possible misconceptions.

Students at practically any level can use Pattern Guides. For example, because we believe that the ability to discover cause-and-effect relationships should be developed at an early age, the Pattern Guide in Figure 46 was created for a primary-level text for a science unit on plants, specifically on seeds (see page 196 in the Appendix for a reproducible version of a Pattern Guide for cause-and-effect relationships). Because primary-level students—and students at all grade levels—enjoy puzzles and manipulative activities, we have adapted the guide to include such activities.

Table 2. Text Pattern Signals

Pattern	Compare and Contrast
Signal Words	but however yet unless while although as well as unless

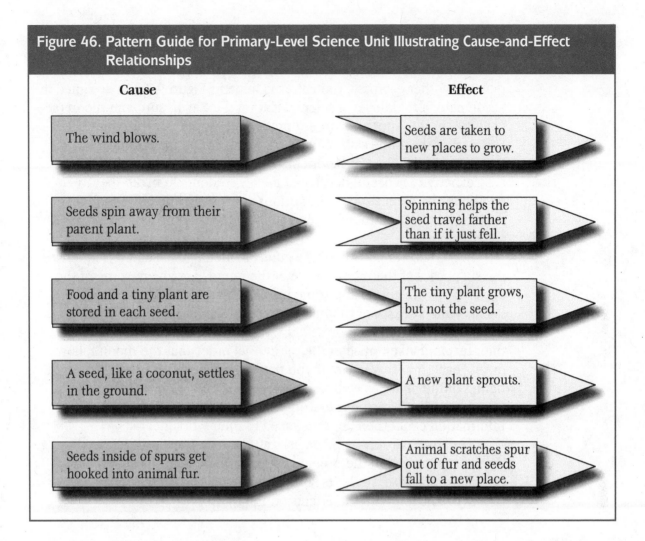

Figure 46. Pattern Guide for Primary-Level Science Unit Illustrating Cause-and-Effect Relationships

Cause	Effect
The wind blows.	Seeds are taken to new places to grow.
Seeds spin away from their parent plant.	Spinning helps the seed travel farther than if it just fell.
Food and a tiny plant are stored in each seed.	The tiny plant grows, but not the seed.
A seed, like a coconut, settles in the ground.	A new plant sprouts.
Seeds inside of spurs get hooked into animal fur.	Animal scratches spur out of fur and seeds fall to a new place.

After reading and discussing the relevant pages in the text, students can work in pairs or groups for the text structure lesson. As noted earlier, the teacher will want to model and thoroughly explain the text pattern to be studied, using everyday examples to show students the value of learning how informational texts are put together. Cause-and-effect puzzle cards are then developed, as illustrated in Figure 46. These are created using different color cards for each category (e.g., red for causes, blue for effects). Laminating the cards will preserve them for repeated use. Page numbers can be written on the back so students know where to look for information in their books. The teacher can tell groups of students to line up their puzzle parts with the causes on the left and the effects on the right. They should first read the information on an "effect" card and try to remember from their reading what the cause was; then they should refer back to the text for confirmation. The teacher can circulate around the groups to assist and assess progress. As a follow-up, we recommend asking the class to point out in their text the line that supports each of their matches. With this activity, the teacher helps students learn not just the information in the content area but how to read this type of material.

In another example, the Pattern Guide in Figure 47 was designed to accompany a middle-level science text on the Earth, sun, and moon (see page 197 in the Appendix for a reproducible version of this guide). The first part of the guide asks students to focus on the main concepts presented in the chapter before beginning the text structure activity. This type of activity is useful because it allows students to make their own decisions and choices about important concepts while helping them develop a cluster of knowledge about significant information on these science concepts.

In the second portion of the guide, students are asked to sequence the six phases of the moon. Some of the names are given, some of the descriptions are given, and some have nothing given. Students must decide which phases of the moon are missing and fill in the missing information in the space provided. This requires students to return to their text and take notice of the sequential order that the moon follows during each monthly cycle. If you prefer working with small groups, the names of the phase as well as a description could be prewritten to sentence strips that students would then use to do a closed sort. This information could then be transferred to their worksheet.

The third part of the guide asks students to draw on their knowledge that was organized in the previous section to determine causes and effects. In this case, students complete a matching exercise, pairing the causes on the left with the effects on the right.

Tips for Diverse Learners

- In order to prevent ELL students from being overwhelmed by the number of terms, introduce them in context, and select a few key terms to introduce at a time.
- Pair an ELL student with another student or tutor.
- Teach concepts as interdisciplinary; when teaching other subjects, be sure to point out key terms learned so that students can see that the text structures can be used in all content areas.

REFERENCES

Herber, H.L. (1970). *Teaching reading in the content areas.* Upper Saddle River, NJ: Prentice Hall.

Vacca, R.T. (1981). *Content area reading.* Boston: Little, Brown.

Vacca, R.T., & Vacca, J.A.L. (2002). *Content area reading: Literacy and learning across the curriculum* (7th ed.). Boston: Allyn & Bacon.

Earth   Sun   Moon

I. Directions: Read the section in your science textbook on "Earth, Sun, and Moon" (pages 530–539). As you read, write three important points relating to each of the following topics.

A. Earth
   1. third planet from the sun
   2. only place in the universe known to have living things
   3. formed 4.57 billion years ago

B. Sun
   1. star at the center of the solar system
   2. one of the brightest stars in the galaxy
   3. primarily composed of hydrogen and helium

C. Moon
   1. Earth's only natural satellite
   2. fifth largest moon in the solar system
   3. orbits Earth every 27.3 days

II. Directions: Using the information given in the text, sequence the phases of the moon. Some of the names or phases are given to you, some of the descriptions of the phases are given, and some have nothing given. You must decide which phases of the moon are missing and fill in the missing information in the space provided using your own words. Remember, there are six true phases of the moon, but you must have seven names and seven descriptions completed in the following chart; there is a space for each phase plus one that is described on your chart.

	Name/Phase of Moon	**Description of Moon**
1	New moon	The moon looks dark because it is between the Earth and sun. The side where light can be seen is facing away from Earth.
2	Waxing crescent	This appears about one week after the new moon. The moon has traveled almost 1/4 around the Earth. About 1/4 of the moon is lighted.
3	First quarter	This appears about one week after the new moon. The moon has traveled almost 1/4 around the Earth. About 1/4 of the moon is lighted.
4	Waxing gibbous	The moon seems to be getting bigger, going from new to crescent to half to gibbous to full.
5	Full moon	The moon's disk is light because the Earth is between the sun and the moon.
6	Waning gibbous	The moon seems to be getting smaller, going from full to gibbous to half to crescent to new.

(continued)

	Name/Phase of Moon	Description of Moon
7	Last quarter (third)	(Also called half moon) when we can see one half of the moon's disk (this is one-quarter of the entire moon's surface).
8	Waning crescent	The moon is now waning, or getting smaller. The lighted portion gets smaller every night until only a thin crescent can be seen.
9	New moon	The moon looks dark because it is between the Earth and sun. The side where light can be seen is facing away from Earth.

III. Directions: From the information you gathered above, we can begin to build connections among various concepts about the Earth, sun, and moon. In this section, we will be examining the causes (why something happens) and the effects (what happened) of science concepts. Match each cause on the left with the appropriate effect on the right by writing the letter of the effect on the appropriate line.

Examples:

Cause

___b___ 1. Reactions in the sun's core release energy.

___a___ 2. Eruptions of gases called solar flares burst from the sun to the Earth.

Effect

A. Beautiful light rays called auroras can be seen from the Earth's poles.

B. Light and heat are provided for the Earth.

Exercise:

Cause

___c___ 1. The sun provides heat and light for the Earth.

___e___ 2. Light from the sun reflects off the moon.

___g___ 3. The moon spins on its axis while it revolves around the Earth one time.

___d___ 4. The moon's shape changes.

___f___ 5. The sun is the center of our solar system.

___a___ 6. The Earth spins from west to east.

___b___ 7. One-half of the Earth is tilted on its axis slightly toward the sun.

Effect

A. The sun always appears to rise in the east and set in the west.

B. Days are longer in the summer and shorter in the winter.

C. Life can be sustained on Earth.

D. The lighted part of the moon we see from Earth changes based on how the moon faces the sun.

E. The moon appears to be lit and shining.

F. Earth and other planets revolve around the sun.

G. We on Earth always see the same side of the moon.

PART VII

Processes-of-Reading Guides

Guides in this section help students simulate the reading process by employing metacognitive skills and strategies. For example, the guides may include activities and inquiries that assist students in selectively attending to only the necessary content in an information source, cueing them to think of analogies, to put information in their own words, or to reread a segment for clarification. These guides can be designed to assist readers in adjusting their reading rate to know when to skim or skip a selection and when to read more thoroughly with a specific purpose in mind.

CHAPTER 19

Glossing

While the use of marginal notes (those written in the margins of a printed text), otherwise known as "glossing," dates back to medieval times (Richgels & Hansen, 1984), Otto, White, Richgels, Hansen, and Morrison (1981) are generally credited with demonstrating how this strategy can be used to improve students' understanding of text. Traditionally, Glossing assists with reading comprehension because it provides a short definition or explanation in the margin for unfamiliar words or concepts (Lomika, 1998). Glossing directs students' attention as they read; teachers can use it to focus on the process of reading (skills and strategies), the content of what is to be read (facts, information, and concepts), or both.

Modifications can be made for Glossing depending on teacher preference. Because most schools forbid marking in textbooks, teachers may feel that it is inappropriate to do standard Glossing because it requires making notations in the text itself. If this is the case, teachers may opt for a version with notations printed on a sort of bookmark and then aligned with the text (this is similar to the Process Guide; see chapter 20). Another version is where Glossing for a text is done during the modeling portion of a lesson on chart paper or on the board; this helps students learn to apply specific strategies or concepts to their own reading material. Glossing also often appears in student journals, on photocopies of printed pages, or on printouts of PDFs or other electronic files.

When using Glossing as a strategy guide for a text, Richgels and Hansen (1984) suggest three general guidelines. The first is to examine the text to determine which skills and strategies are needed to maximize comprehension. Strong readers point to four strategies as the most useful in reading content area texts: establishing a purpose for reading, relating the content to prior knowledge, organizing the newly read information, and monitoring one's own comprehension (Otto et al., 1981).

Grade Levels
Intermediate, middle, secondary

Subjects
Reading/language arts, social studies, science, fine arts

Classroom Contexts
Individuals, small groups, whole class, tutoring sessions

Teacher-created Glossing notes can help engage students in using these strategies, as illustrated in Figure 48. In this example, a teacher created an expository text for students to read to support their textbook reading and reiterate key vocabulary terms of the unit. The list was created as a whole-group think-aloud during a shared reading; key questions the teacher wanted students to remember while reading were posted on the board. These questions were discussed as a whole group before reading began and were also available for students to refer back to during the reading. Examples of these questions included Where do ants live? How do they talk with each other? and What do they do for work? Glossing lists could be modified to a written form for more advanced studies, a form similar to an Anticipation Guide (see chapter 11). As the unit progresses, the teacher can place more responsibility on the students and oversee the transition in Glossing from a verbal activity to a prewriting activity.

Another guideline for using Glossing as a strategy guide is to be aware of students' levels of understanding. Students who have difficulty understanding content area vocabulary will need notations that explain meanings in straightforward terms. At times textbook authors erroneously assume that readers possess the prior knowledge necessary to understand new concepts; when this happens, teachers can use Glossing notation to provide the extra information or explanation needed. In Figure 48, the teacher used Glossing to highlight the key vocabulary words. Because the text was created by the teacher in order to reiterate important information students may have missed when they read from their textbooks, the definitions of the vocabulary terms were already written in the students' journals. A quick review of the definitions they wrote prior to this shared reading and a statement during the Glossing that this is one of the three text features used in the text should be all that is necessary for Glossing the terms.

Finally, it is important to be aware of the physical and personal realities of the classroom environment. Make certain that the Glossing notations are brief and used only when necessary to meet lesson objectives. If used when not needed, struggling readers will only have more text to wade through while attempting to comprehend what they are reading. The Glossing example shown in Figure 49 was developed for a Robert Frost poem studied in a secondary-level English language arts classroom. Here the Glossing is used to focus instruction on questioning and evaluating.

While working with a copy of the poem on the overhead or chart paper, the teacher made a copy for each student to jot their notes on instead of having to do so in a separate journal. With the poem being four stanzas, the teacher decided to scaffold the instruction for a shared reading. When working with the first paragraph, the teacher alone uses

Figure 48. Glossing Notes for Primary-Level Text on Ants

Directions for teachers: Read through the following Glossing list with students for the text titled "Ants" while doing a shared reading; spend more time when necessary.

Text for Shared Reading

"Ants"

Home
Ants. They are everywhere. Ants live and work together in **colonies**. A **colony** is like a big city. Most colonies live in **tunnels** underground. Ants carry out dirt from the tunnels and the dirt forms a pile called an anthill.

Communication
Like other insects, ants have two **antennae**. Antennae are like noses and fingers. They use them to smell and feel what is going on around them. Ants **communicate** with each other by rubbing their antennae together.

Work
Ants are small, but they work together on big jobs. They are experts on **teamwork**. A bunch of little ants can carry a big dead bug back to the colony. Ants can even build a bridge to cross between tree branches. They hold onto each other's legs and other ants walk across to the new branch.

Oral Glossing List (to be done during Shared Reading of above text)

Establishing Purpose
- As you read, note several characteristics of ants in your journal.
- After reading this section, you should be able to identify where ants live, how they talk with each other, and what they do for work.

Using Prior Knowledge
- Where have you seen ants? What have you observed ants doing?
- List what comes to your mind when you think of ants.

Organizing New Information
- What three text features are used in this text? What does each mean?

Monitoring Comprehension
- Answer the following questions:
  1. What are colonies?
  2. If ants did not have antennae they would not be able to (list at least one thing mentioned in the passage)_____.
- How certain are you of your above answers? You may go back to the text to check your answers if you are unsure of them.

#1	sure	not sure
#2	sure	not sure

Figure 49. Glossing for Secondary English Language Arts Lesson on Robert Frost's "The Road Not Taken"

(English—Secondary Text)

Directions for teachers: Pass out copies of the text. Read the text orally at least one time to the class before beginning the Glossing section (it is important for students to hear the text before they begin to take it apart). On the overhead or chart paper, decide as a class which symbols will signify vocabulary words, places to question and evaluate, what signifies where clarification needs to be made, and what signifies any questions brought up due to reading the text. The first stanza will be done by the teacher as a model, the second as a whole class, the third in partners, and the fourth individually.

Poem Title: "The Road Not Taken" by Robert Frost

Two roads diverged in a yellow wood,
And sorry I could not travel both
And be one traveler, long I stood
And looked down one as far as I could.
To where it bent in the undergrowth,

Then took the other, as just as fair,
And having perhaps the better claim,
Because it was grassy and wanted wear,
Though as for that, the passing there
Had worn them really about the same,

And both that morning equally lay
In leaves no step had trodden black.
Oh, I kept the first for another day!
Yet knowing how way leads on to way
I doubted if I should ever come back.

I shall be telling this with a sigh
Somewhere ages and ages hence:
Two roads diverged in a wood, and I—
I took the one less traveled by,
And that has made all the difference.

Glossing Notes

> KEY
>
> **V** = Vocabulary
> ←   Go back to the beginning of sentence/stanza and reword in common terms
> **E** = Evaluate this line
> **C** = Clarify

I do:
Two roads diverged **V** in a yellow wood,
And sorry I could not travel both **E**
And be one traveler, **C** long I stood
And looked down one as far as I could. ←
To where it bent in the undergrowth, **V**

We do:
Then took the other, as just as fair, **V**
And having perhaps **V** the better claim, **C**
Because it was grassy and wanted wear, **E**
Though as for that, **C** the passing there
Had worn them really about the same, ←

> **Stanza 1**
> **V** <u>diverge</u>—branch out/off, extend in different directions
> **E** Why might you want to travel both? Could both roads be good?
> **C** The author is alone.
> ← The author comes across two roads going different directions in the woods. He is traveling alone, but wishes he could travel both. Standing there he looks down one as far as he could see.
> **V** <u>undergrowth</u>—small trees and brush; low-growing plants

"The Road Not Taken" from *The Poetry of Robert Frost* edited by Edward Connery Lathem. Copyright 1916, 1969 by Henry Holt and Company. Copyright 1944 by Robert Frost. Reprinted by permission of Henry Holt and Company, LLC.

Glossing. The second stanza is completed as a whole group by following key Glossing symbols used in the class. Figure 49 illustrates the use of these symbols for the first and second stanzas as completed first by the teacher and then by the whole class. These two stanzas are labeled according to who will be doing it; a key is clearly posted showing the four focuses for the lesson (vocabulary, clarifying, evaluating, and checking comprehension). The third stanza is completed in pairs, and the fourth is completed individually and finally checked by a partner. By breaking the process down like this, the teacher is gradually handing over the instruction to the students; they are Glossing the poem to aid their own comprehension. A sample of what the Glossing notes could look like for stanza 1 appears at the end of Figure 49.

Tips for Diverse Learners

- Before assigning text, frontload vocabulary and instruct students to point to and say each new word.
- Pair an ELL student with another student/tutor.
- Use key symbols to signify certain tasks (e.g., circle vocabulary words, put a question mark next to phrases to examine significance, underline text features).

REFERENCES

Lomika, L. (1998). "To gloss or not to gloss": An investigation of reading comprehension online. *Language Learning & Technology, 1*(2), 41–50.

Otto, W., White, S., Richgels, D.J., Hansen, R., & Morrison, B. (1981). *A technique for improving the understanding of expository text: Gloss and examples* (Theoretical Paper No. 96). Madison: Wisconsin Center for Education Research.

Richgels, D.J., & Hansen, R. (1984). Gloss: Helping students apply both skills and strategies in reading content texts. *Journal of Reading, 27*, 312–317.

LITERATURE CITED

Frost, R. (1969). The road not taken. In Lathem, E.C. (Ed.), *The poetry of Robert Frost* (p. 105). New York: Henry Holt.

CHAPTER 20

Process Guide

Karlin (1964) designed the Process Guide to help students identify the comprehension skills necessary to master specific content. This guide is best used with a print-based text due to the bookmark format. According to Karlin, a Process Guide can cover several skill areas, including recognizing text structure, making inferences, identifying important information, evaluating content, and using context clues. The Process Guide is similar to Glossing (see chapter 19) except that it does not require marking the actual text because the guide is created in the form of a supplementary bookmark. Therefore, unlike other strategy guides in this book, the Process Guide is not to be created on regular-sized paper but is instead printed on a strip of paper meant to resemble a bookmark and is aligned with students' texts. The bookmark format of the Process Guide makes this a preferred strategy guide among teachers (see page 199 in the Appendix for a reproducible version of the Process Guide Bookmark).

This guide can be used at any grade level and in any content area. Used while studying poetry in language arts, it directs students' attention to structural features such as similes, metaphors, contrasts, and alliterations. In other subjects, it can be used to point out certain keywords and their definitions or to signal students to make predictions, draw conclusions, find the main idea, or ponder an idea. It can also be used to point out the main idea of a paragraph, the text structure or pattern used, when information is implied rather than directly stated, and other aspects of writing. The focus of the Process Guides should be on the most significant information from each passage. Teachers can ask questions, present various tasks to be undertaken, or point out particular areas for students to focus on.

The flexible purpose of Process Guides allows them to be used in a variety of ways. Because they are in the form of a bookmark, they can be

Grade Levels
Intermediate, middle, secondary

Subjects
Reading/language arts, social studies, science, fine arts

Classroom Contexts
Individuals, small groups, whole class, tutoring sessions

Guiding Readers Through Text: Strategy Guides for New Times (2nd ed.) by Karen D. Wood, Diane Lapp, James Flood, and D. Bruce Taylor. © 2008 by the International Reading Association.

kept in the students' text to refresh their memories of certain passages or they can be gathered and stored together for studying longer units. When working with a partner, students can use key concepts from the Process Guide bookmarks to trigger more elaborate associations from their reading and class discussions. Once the teacher feels comfortable that students are beginning to understand how to select key concepts, he or she can instruct students to develop their own Process Guides, either independently or in pairs.

In Figure 50 we show how the Process Guide can be used with younger students who are becoming acquainted with vocabulary on character traits. Using ideas based on an article by Manyak (2007), the Process Guide bookmark was used to introduce five new character trait vocabulary words during a daily read-aloud of *James and the Giant Peach* by Roald Dahl in a second-grade classroom. For this lesson, the bookmark-like cards were prepared in advance with the character names and five new character trait vocabulary words on them, as the teacher would predetermine which characters count as main characters and which do not. In this case the main characters are as follows: James, Aunt

---

Figure 50. Process Guide for Primary-Level Lesson on Character Traits

James and the Giant Peach

	Bold	Conceited	Irritable	Insensitive	Supportive
James					
Aunt Spiker					
Aunt Sponge					
Centipede					
Earthworm					
Glowworm					
Grasshopper					
Miss Spider					
Ladybug					

Sponge, Aunt Spiker, Centipede, Grasshopper, Miss Spider, Earthworm, Glowworm, and Ladybug. The five character trait vocabulary words selected from Manyak's suggested list are *bold, conceited, irritable, insensitive,* and *supportive*. Students were instructed to illustrate their favorite character of the book on one side of the bookmark and were reminded to keep the illustration close to how the character is described by the author. On the other side of the bookmark, students were instructed to check off the vocabulary words that describe the character.

It is important to use the vocabulary listed on the Process Guide bookmark regularly in class discussions so that students become accustomed to it. Students can keep these bookmarks for future reference so that, as they continue reading the book, they can refer to them to record new major character names. By keeping track of the main characters on a bookmark, students will be able to refer back to it for cues on the character. The bookmark can also be kept as part of a set on character trait vocabulary words; if five new traits are chosen for each book, then students can use the bookmarks to review meanings of the vocabulary throughout the year.

Figure 51 illustrates the use of a Process Guide with a graphic novel. The secondary students were learning about the Constitutional Convention of 1787 (also known as the Philadelphia Convention), and the teacher opted to use a graphic novel chapter about this topic to support the history textbook. The material discussed in the graphic novel reviews already learned information; however, the material is presented through a modern-day medium—the graphic novel—with which most students are very accustomed. The hope in reviewing the material in a different fashion than it was originally taught is that it will make the information appear more real and relevant to their lives.

In this Process Guide, students will fill in the blanks by reading the graphic novel in groups of six. Because there are six characters in the graphic novel, each group member will be assigned to reading the part of one character (Reporter, Professor Williamson, Benjamin Franklin, Alexander Hamilton, James Madison, and George Washington). The text can be read through several times, because it is fairly short, to ensure correct answers are recorded on the Process Guide. Once the guide is completed, students can refer back to their textbook to verify their answers. The Process Guide used with the graphic novel in this lesson can also be transferred to the textbook, as both are discussing the same topic. This Process Guide bookmark can be kept as a quick review or overview of the Philadelphia Convention, or Constitutional Convention, before the unit exam.

Figure 51. Process Guide for Intermediate-Level History Lesson on the Philadelphia Convention

The Philadelphia Convention of 1787

What were the four proposals presented at this convention to form a new government?

1. (Virginia Plan)
2. (New Jersey Plan)
3. (Hamilton's Plan)
4. (Dickinson's Plan)

Of the now 50 states, how many were originally present during the convention? 13

How many delegates were involved in the decision? 55

In your words, what occurred during Shays' rebellion? Farmers refused to pay what they believed were unfair taxes.

How did the convention shape modern day America? Creation of the United States Constitution.

Tips for Diverse Learners

- Pair ELL students with another student/tutor.
- Before assigning text, frontload vocabulary and instruct students to point to and say each new word.
- When able, incorporate pictures with vocabulary words and use word banks.

REFERENCES

Karlin, R. (1964). *Teaching reading in high school*. Indianapolis, IN: Bobbs-Merrill.

Manyak, P. (2007). Character trait vocabulary: A schoolwide approach. *The Reading Teacher, 60*, 574–577.

CHAPTER 21

Reading Road Map

One assumption underlying the Reading Road Map (described in Buehl, 2001; Wood, 1988; Wood & Harmon, 2001) is that the poor comprehenders tend to read all material at the same rate—either very quickly or very slowly and deliberately. Based on this assumption, the Reading Road Map guides students through the content by helping them adjust their reading rate to correspond with the importance of the concepts encountered. A typical Reading Road Map comprises missions (interspersed questions and activities), road signs (reading rate indicators), and location signs (headings and page or paragraph numbers). Students can choose or be assigned a "traveling companion" for their journey through the text. Most teachers elect to have students write their answers on separate sheets of paper, preserving the guides for subsequent classes.

Because this approach is novel, it tends to capture the attention of students who are difficult to motivate. It can be modified and used at any grade level, although in the secondary years, it is probably most appropriate for the remedial or resource room setting. As with any guide, it is important to thoroughly explain the purpose of the Reading Road Map. Parallels can be drawn between the "textbook journey" and an actual trip to another location. In reading, as with travel, it is much less confusing to look ahead, plan your course, and know where you are going before you get there. An introduction such as the following should pique interest:

> We have discussed how difficult it can be to read and thoroughly understand all of the new information in our textbooks and other sources. So, instead of just reading the next chapter, we are going on a tour together—a tour of the world of arthropods. We'll stop along the way to take a closer look at some of the things we find. Oh, and I have made a map for us to use. We'll skim it first to get an idea of what we will see before we actually make the journey. Then we'll be off!

Grade Levels
Primary, intermediate, middle, secondary

Subjects
Reading/language arts, English, social studies, science, fine arts

Classroom Contexts
Individuals, small groups, whole class

Guiding Readers Through Text: Strategy Guides for New Times (2nd ed.) by Karen D. Wood, Diane Lapp, James Flood, and D. Bruce Taylor. © 2008 by the International Reading Association.

The Reading Road Map shown in Figure 52 guides intermediate-level students through a chapter on arthropods. While not illustrated by the figure, to build background knowledge and assist the students in creating visual images while reading, the teacher began the lesson by taking the students on a virtual tour of the evolution of the arthropod by guiding them through an article on the Understanding Evolution website called "The Arthropod Story" online at evolution.berkeley.edu/evolibrary/article/_0_0/arthropodstory. The teacher told the students to use information learned from this virtual experience along with the textbook content as they answer the guide questions. For example, for question 4A in Figure 52, which asks, "How would you know a crustacean if you saw one? Where would you look for one?" two students working together using information from both the text and the virtual tour that preceded the reading responded as follows:

> Well, not all of the crustaceans we learned about are as big as shrimp, lobsters, crayfish, and crabs. The tour we took said there are crustaceans that are less than a centimeter long and there are so many of them in the ocean, they outweigh all the whales. We would know crustaceans when we saw them because they have three body parts: the head, thorax, and abdomen, and they are hard on the outside.

Students engage in a variety of activities along the way including retelling, recalling, outlining, and comparing. The traveling companions can take turns reading portions of the text and deciding on the most logical answers. The teacher may intervene at various points during the journey to provide additional explanations or to request comments from the students. The last "mission" in this guide is for students to think back on the trip to recall whatever they can about the four types of arthropods described in the chapter. This type of mental review aids long-term recall. Teachers can also use the study guide to teach this strategy and then instruct students to apply the mental review process independently with later reading assignments.

The Reading Road Map in Figure 53 was designed for a middle school science lesson on pollution. Notice how the students are asked to go beyond the textbook to websites to respond and expand their thinking and to use the Internet to research information about current restrictions on pesticides. The following is a sample response of two students working together to research question 11C in Figure 53:

> DDT started to be banned in 1962 when a book came out called *Silent Spring* by an American biologist named Rachel Carson. She said that because DDT was used so much to kill mosquitoes, it was causing cancer in people and killing lots of birds and wildlife. The wikipedia article said since DDT was banned we are seeing more bald eagles around, which were on the endangered species list before.

Figure 52. Reading Road Map for Intermediate-Level Lesson on Arthropods

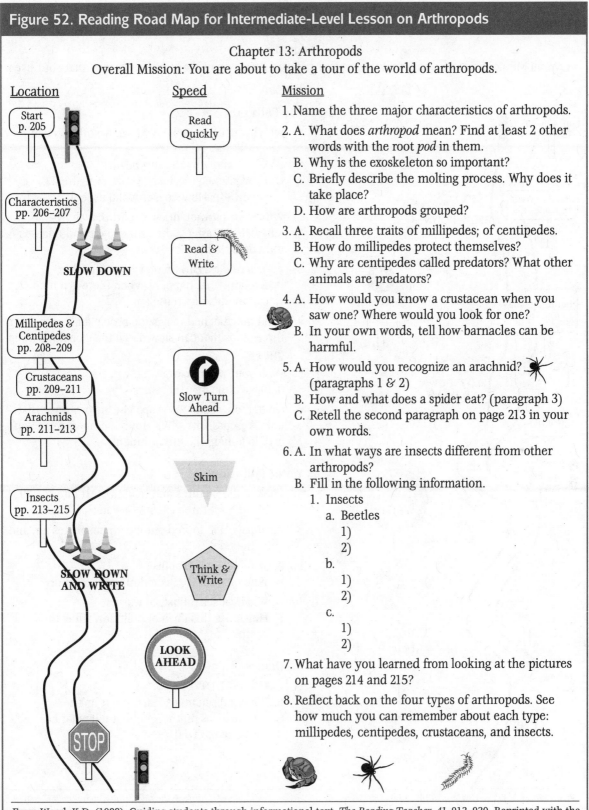

Chapter 13: Arthropods
Overall Mission: You are about to take a tour of the world of arthropods.

Location

Start
p. 205

Characteristics
pp. 206–207

SLOW DOWN

Millipedes &
Centipedes
pp. 208–209

Crustaceans
pp. 209–211

Arachnids
pp. 211–213

Insects
pp. 213–215

SLOW DOWN
AND WRITE

STOP

Speed

Read
Quickly

Read &
Write

Slow Turn
Ahead

Skim

Think &
Write

LOOK
AHEAD

Mission

1. Name the three major characteristics of arthropods.
2. A. What does *arthropod* mean? Find at least 2 other words with the root *pod* in them.
   B. Why is the exoskeleton so important?
   C. Briefly describe the molting process. Why does it take place?
   D. How are arthropods grouped?
3. A. Recall three traits of millipedes; of centipedes.
   B. How do millipedes protect themselves?
   C. Why are centipedes called predators? What other animals are predators?
4. A. How would you know a crustacean when you saw one? Where would you look for one?
   B. In your own words, tell how barnacles can be harmful.
5. A. How would you recognize an arachnid? (paragraphs 1 & 2)
   B. How and what does a spider eat? (paragraph 3)
   C. Retell the second paragraph on page 213 in your own words.
6. A. In what ways are insects different from other arthropods?
   B. Fill in the following information.
      1. Insects
         a. Beetles
            1)
            2)
         b.
            1)
            2)
         c.
            1)
            2)
7. What have you learned from looking at the pictures on pages 214 and 215?
8. Reflect back on the four types of arthropods. See how much you can remember about each type: millipedes, centipedes, crustaceans, and insects.

From Wood, K.D. (1988). Guiding students through informational text. *The Reading Teacher, 41*, 912–920. Reprinted with the permission of the International Reading Association.

Figure 53. Reading Road Map for Middle-Level Lesson on Pollution

Pollution

Overall Mission: You are about to learn how air pollution, water pollution, and pesticides affect our lives.

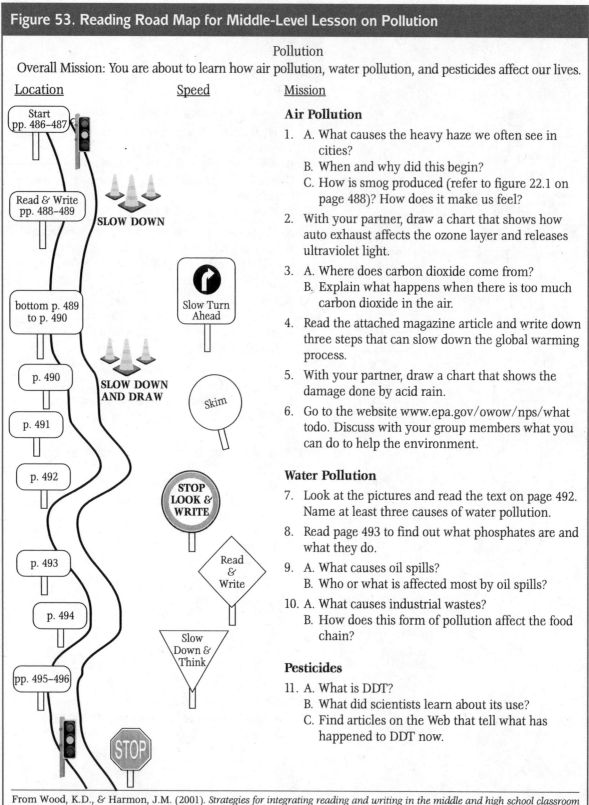

Location | Speed | Mission

Air Pollution

1. A. What causes the heavy haze we often see in cities?
   B. When and why did this begin?
   C. How is smog produced (refer to figure 22.1 on page 488)? How does it make us feel?

2. With your partner, draw a chart that shows how auto exhaust affects the ozone layer and releases ultraviolet light.

3. A. Where does carbon dioxide come from?
   B. Explain what happens when there is too much carbon dioxide in the air.

4. Read the attached magazine article and write down three steps that can slow down the global warming process.

5. With your partner, draw a chart that shows the damage done by acid rain.

6. Go to the website www.epa.gov/owow/nps/what todo. Discuss with your group members what you can do to help the environment.

Water Pollution

7. Look at the pictures and read the text on page 492. Name at least three causes of water pollution.

8. Read page 493 to find out what phosphates are and what they do.

9. A. What causes oil spills?
   B. Who or what is affected most by oil spills?

10. A. What causes industrial wastes?
    B. How does this form of pollution affect the food chain?

Pesticides

11. A. What is DDT?
    B. What did scientists learn about its use?
    C. Find articles on the Web that tell what has happened to DDT now.

Location road map labels: Start pp. 486–487; Read & Write pp. 488–489; bottom p. 489 to p. 490; p. 490; p. 491; p. 492; p. 493; p. 494; pp. 495–496

Speed signs: SLOW DOWN; Slow Turn Ahead; SLOW DOWN AND DRAW; Skim; STOP LOOK & WRITE; Read & Write; Slow Down & Think; STOP

From Wood, K.D., & Harmon, J.M. (2001). *Strategies for integrating reading and writing in the middle and high school classroom* (pp. 88–89). Westerville, OH: National Middle School Association. Adapted with the permission of the National Middle School Association.

The Reading Road Map excerpt in Figure 54 was developed by University of North Carolina at Charlotte preservice teachers Schuyler Quinley, Alicia Jones, Shannon Burpeau, and Jessica Bridges for an assignment in their undergraduate reading methods course. They developed an intermediate-level guide on the Industrial Revolution that takes students to related websites, asks them to make charts of the inventions and their inventor, and instructs them to write in their journals, take on the perspective of a Cherokee Indian during the Trail of

Figure 54. Excerpt from Reading Road Map for Intermediate-Level Lesson on the Industrial Revolution

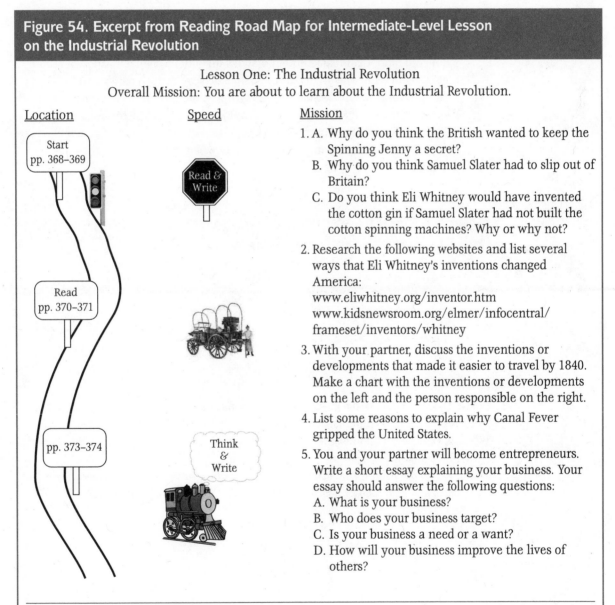

Lesson One: The Industrial Revolution
Overall Mission: You are about to learn about the Industrial Revolution.

Location

Start
pp. 368–369

Read
pp. 370–371

pp. 373–374

Speed

Read & Write

Think & Write

Mission

1. A. Why do you think the British wanted to keep the Spinning Jenny a secret?
   B. Why do you think Samuel Slater had to slip out of Britain?
   C. Do you think Eli Whitney would have invented the cotton gin if Samuel Slater had not built the cotton spinning machines? Why or why not?

2. Research the following websites and list several ways that Eli Whitney's inventions changed America:
   www.eliwhitney.org/inventor.htm
   www.kidsnewsroom.org/elmer/infocentral/frameset/inventors/whitney

3. With your partner, discuss the inventions or developments that made it easier to travel by 1840. Make a chart with the inventions or developments on the left and the person responsible on the right.

4. List some reasons to explain why Canal Fever gripped the United States.

5. You and your partner will become entrepreneurs. Write a short essay explaining your business. Your essay should answer the following questions:
   A. What is your business?
   B. Who does your business target?
   C. Is your business a need or a want?
   D. How will your business improve the lives of others?

Created by preservice teachers Schuyler Quinley, Alicia Jones, Jessica Bridges, and Shannon Burpeau of the University of North Carolina at Charlotte, USA. Reprinted with permission.

Tears, develop a map of their journey, create a flag for Texas, and design a real-estate ad bringing new people to the state during the Gold Rush, to name a few of the engaging activities. This guide can lead students through an entire unit on the Industrial Revolution with students spending a portion of a class period on the guide and its activities over the course of several weeks. Because it incorporates so many of the processes associated with developing effective and strategic readers, it is an excellent choice for a blocked schedule of social studies and language arts, for example. Students working together on Question 2 researched the websites and came up with the following response:

> One way his invention changed America is that everybody wanted a cotton gin and it helped us turn out millions of dollars of profit for the cotton planters. Our book just talked about Eli Whitney inventing the cotton gin, but he did more than that. Another way his inventions changed America is that he figured out how to make rifle parts faster by doing a pattern and making several at a time. That way, they would not have to be handmade from stock to barrel. So, it was because of Eli Whitney that factories started. Also, we found out that many people stole his idea for the cotton gin and that patents only allow you to sue somebody who steals your idea, they don't prevent them from doing it.

Tips for Diverse Learners

- Thoroughly model and think aloud examples.
- Make sure partners can mutually benefit from working together.
- Include activities that involve pictorial information.
- Encourage labeling of key concepts.

REFERENCES

Buehl, D. (2001). *Classroom strategies for interactive learning* (2nd ed.). Newark, DE: International Reading Association.

Wood, K.D. (1988). Guiding students through informational text. *The Reading Teacher, 41*, 912–920.

Wood, K.D., & Harmon, J.M. (2001). *Strategies for integrating reading and writing in the middle and high school classroom*. Westerville, OH: National Middle School Association.

CHAPTER 22

Textbook Activity Guide

Davey's (1986) Textbook Activity Guide (TAG) is based on research in metacognition and therefore has a self-monitoring component (Allen, 2004; Johns & Lenski, 2005). The TAG provides a set of strategy codes that directs students to complete a specific type of activity for each portion read; for instance, students may make predictions about a selection, discuss the text with a partner, retell or write a response to information, or draw diagrams or maps. The guide also includes self-monitoring codes that allow students to indicate which portions of the selections need further clarification. Davey's research has shown that TAGs enhance students' overall learning by helping them become active, independent learners who monitor their reading, reflect on the content, and identify points that require rereading on their own part or additional clarification from the teacher, an additional online resource, or even another student.

Developing a TAG involves four steps. First, go through the selection and pick out the headings, portions, and diagrams that relate to your objectives. Next select which text features you want to use in the study guide and sequence them appropriately. The third step involves matching the reading task to the objective (this is where the strategy codes come in). When the objective calls for inferencing or brainstorming of prior knowledge, the most appropriate task might be to discuss the selection with a partner. When you want students to sequence, organize, or show relationships, having them make a chart or diagram is a logical approach. Choose one task for each text portion on your guide. The fourth step in developing a TAG is to create a self-monitoring system that is understandable and helpful to students. Line markers can be placed beside each numbered task for students to indicate their level of understanding. This way, the teacher can walk around the class to see which areas may require additional review or explanation.

Grade Levels
Intermediate, middle, secondary

Subjects
Science, language arts, social studies, fine arts

Classroom Contexts
Individuals, pairs

Guiding Readers Through Text: Strategy Guides for New Times (2nd ed.) by Karen D. Wood, Diane Lapp, James Flood, and D. Bruce Taylor. © 2008 by the International Reading Association.

When first implemented, work on the TAG should last approximately one class period; the guide itself should therefore be fairly short. As students gain proficiency in their use, the TAGs can be lengthened and their use can span several class periods. Because TAGS will be new to the students, the introduction of the guide to the class should involve much explanation on the part of the teacher. Begin by clarifying the lesson objectives for the chapter, online source, or text segment under study. Then, students can be assigned to work in pairs to complete this strategy guide. Don't forget to emphasize why you are using these guides; it is important that students understand the TAG's value as a self-evaluation strategy to enhance their learning.

Figure 55 is a Textbook Activity Guide for a middle-level science class on the topic of "fossils." While this guide is developed on a text chapter, students can be easily guided to seek out information from other sources. Note how the last assignment requires that students examine and comment on the fossil collection available in the classroom. This TAG helps students monitor their comprehension by having them indicate—with a check mark, a question mark, or an X—the degree to which they understand a particular question or segment of text. Strategy codes are explained at the top of the guide and placed beside each question to cue the desired type of response (teachers can change or add strategy codes as needed for a given lesson). Note how Question 1 asks students to survey the text selection with their partners. Surveying a chapter is a good way to "ground" the subsequent reading and to build a framework for connecting new knowledge; including this step on a guide is one way to help students develop this strategy independently.

Tips for Diverse Learners

- Pair an ELL student with another student or tutor for reading and discussing.
- When brainstorming and discussing, make sure that all students are familiar with key concepts and text structures.

REFERENCES

Allen, J. (2004). *Tools for teaching content literacy*. Portland, ME: Stenhouse.

Davey, B. (1986). Using textbook activity guides to help students learn from textbooks. *Journal of Reading, 29*, 489–494.

Johns, J.L., & Lenski, S.D. (2005). *Improving reading: Strategies and resources* (4th ed.). Dubuque, IA: Kendall/Hunt.

Wood, K.D., & Harmon, J.M. (2001). *Strategies for integrating reading and writing in the middle and high school classroom*. Westerville, OH: National Middle School Association.

Figure 55. Textbook Activity Guide for Middle-Level Science Lesson on Fossils

Textbook Activity Guide

Strategy Codes

RR- Read and retell in your own words
DP- Read and discuss with your partner
PP- Predict with a partner
WR- Write a response on your own

Skim- Read quickly for purpose stated and discuss with partner
MOC- Organize information with a map, chart, or outline

Self-Monitoring Codes:

☑ I understand this information.
? I'm not sure if I understand.
☒ I do not understand and I need to restudy.

1. _____PP pp. 385–392. Survey the title, picture, charts, and headings. What do you expect to learn about this selection?

2. _____WR As you are reading, jot down three or more new words and definitions for your vocabulary collection.

3. _____RR pp. 385–386, first three paragraphs

4. _____DP pp. 386–387, next three paragraphs
    1. Describe several reasons why index or guide fossils are important.
    2. How can finding the right type of fossil help you identify it?

5. _____MOC Map pp. 387–389. Make an outline of the information.
    1. _____   2. _____   3. _____
      a. _____   a. _____   a. _____
      b. _____   b. _____   b. _____
      c. _____   c. _____   c. _____

6. _____Skim p. 390, first three paragraphs
Purpose: To understand the role of the following in the formation of fossils
_____ a. natural casts
_____ b. trails and burrows
_____ c. gastroliths

7. _____DP pp. 390–391
As an amateur fossil collector, describe:
a. where to find fossils
b. what to use to find them
c. how to prepare them for display

8. _____WR p. 392, next to the last paragraph
Define *pseudofossil*. Jot down three other words that contain the prefix *pseudo*. Use the dictionary as necessary.

9. _____DP Examine the website www.geocities.com "Fossil collections of the world" and discuss at least five new things you learned.

Adapted from Wood, K.D., & Harmon, J.M. (2001). *Strategies for integrating reading and writing in the middle and high school classroom* (p. 86). Westerville, OH: National Middle School Association. Adapted with the permission of the National Middle School Association.

PART VIII

Transferring to Independent Learning

Now that your students have mastered specific learning strategies through the use of the strategy guides in this book, it is important to teach them how to apply these strategies on their own. In this final section of the book, you will learn how the Student-Developed Guide can help transfer your students toward independent learning and comprehension strategy use. You will also learn how the notion of a Student-Developed Guide can be adapted and modified according to the variations in individual learning styles.

Student-Developed Guide

The Student-Developed Guide is the last one in the book because it represents one of the latter phases in the journey to independent reading and learning—individual practice. As was mentioned in chapter 1 with the introduction of the Phased Transfer Model, the end goal with using strategy guides is to make the use of guides obsolete and to create strategic readers who are more proficient at attending to the most significant information from printed sources. In particular, the use of a Student-Developed Guide has been advocated for use with struggling readers who are frequently overwhelmed by large amounts of print (Wood & Beattie, 2004). When the teacher feels students have had sufficient practice and proficiency while using one or more of the guide variations mentioned in this text, students can take responsibility over their learning by developing their own guide while reading assigned material.

As with any other guide mentioned in the book, the Student-Developed Guide is not limited solely to textbook reading. This guide can be used for viewed information, online sources, websites, Internet encyclopedia entries, and any other material relevant to course content and assignments. With Student-Developed Guides, like many other strategy guides, students are asked to read the text in segments or chunks. However, instead of being asked a teacher-developed question, they are instructed to ask themselves, What did I just read here? Depending upon the type of material, teachers may tell the students to use the subheadings as aids in the development of their guides by turning the subheading into a question. This practice has been advocated in the professional literature for decades beginning with Robinson's (1946)

Grade Levels
Elementary, intermediate, middle, secondary

Subjects
Science, language arts, social studies, fine arts

Classroom Contexts
Individuals, pairs

Guiding Readers Through Text: Strategy Guides for New Times (2nd ed.) by Karen D. Wood, Diane Lapp, James Flood, and D. Bruce Taylor. © 2008 by the International Reading Association.

well-known study strategy, Survey, Question, Read, Recite, and Review, or SQ3R as it is commonly called (Taylor & Wood, 2005). Numerous adaptations of this study strategy have appeared through the years, including the more recent THIEVES (Manz, 2002) strategy. For the THIEVES strategy, students are told to "steal" information before, during, and after reading by using the following steps:

- **T**itle. What do I know about the topic?

- **H**eadings. Turn the heading into a question and find the answer in the next paragraphs.

- **I**ntroduction. What do I already know, and what else does the introduction tell me?

- **E**very first sentence of each paragraph. Read these sentences and try to get a sense of what the chapter is about.

- **V**isuals and vocabulary. What do the maps, charts, graphs, pictures, boldfaced or italicized print tell me?

- **E**nd-of-chapter question. What do I need to pay attention to while reading?

- **S**ummary. Read and rewrite it in your own words.

Depending upon the level of scaffolding needed for individual students, the teacher might (a) decide to pair students to work together for this activity before instructing them to develop a guide on their own and (b) design a "generic, transitional guide" before instructing them to develop a guide solely on their own. In Figure 56, a guide created by a middle school student for an American history unit, the teacher handed out a form as a "generic" strategy guide with a place for the headings, the page numbers, and some suggested areas of focus in the left-hand column. The information in the left-hand column serves like a bookmark to remind the students while reading to focus on some of the important concepts, facts, dates, and people and to continually ask questions while reading. It also gives them choices of what to focus on and how to respond to the content. Other suggestions to the students might include asking them to develop images, share analogies, or put the information in their own words. In this example, the student wrote down the page numbers and turned the subheadings of the text into questions. Then the student read the segment, reviewed the information, and jotted down the most significant content in the right-hand column. Afterward, the student was able to use the guide to review for the subsequent test. Instead of the student looking back over pages and pages of printed material, the Student-Developed Guide provides a condensed version written largely in the student's own words and using abbreviated, unstilted language.

For a high school lesson on anxiety and depression for a health class, one student strategically placed sticky notes on textbook pages being

Figure 56. Student-Developed Guide for Middle School Lesson on American History

Pages	Subheading
228-229	Why Were There Growing Markets?
New terms/dates/ reminds me of/ important information/ questions/ Internet sources	Steamboats and railroads helped ship grain in Ohio to the eastern states. Railroads helped <u>markets</u> all over where people can buy and sell things.
229-230	Why Were There More and More Cities?
New terms/dates/ reminds me of/ important information/ questions/ Internet sources	Railroad and canals helped transport goods. Cities grew because the people could get other products. <u>DeWitt Clinton</u>, politician, mostly responsible for creating Erie Canal Steam locomotive named after him began in 1831-early train went 16 mph <u>How fast do trains go today?</u> Fastest train is from France and it goes 357 mph (Internet source www.iht.com/articles/2007/04/03/news/train.ph)
230	How Did Industries Get a Boost?
New terms/dates/ reminds me of/ important information/ questions Internet sources	Things weren't made by hand like guns used to be. <u>Eli Whitney</u> came up with a machine for <u>interchangeable parts</u> (parts that can be used for more than one thing) to make lots of one part.

From Wood, K.D., & Beattie, J. (2004). Meeting the literacy needs of students with ADHD in the middle school classroom. *Middle School Journal*, 35(3), 50–55. Reprinted with the permission of the National Middle School Association.

studied to mark the concepts the student felt were most significant. For example, at the place in the book where anxiety was discussed, the student wrote on a sticky note, "Feeling anxious is natural and normal" and placed the sticky note in the appropriate location in the book. After writing on the sticky notes, the student in this example organized the notes under

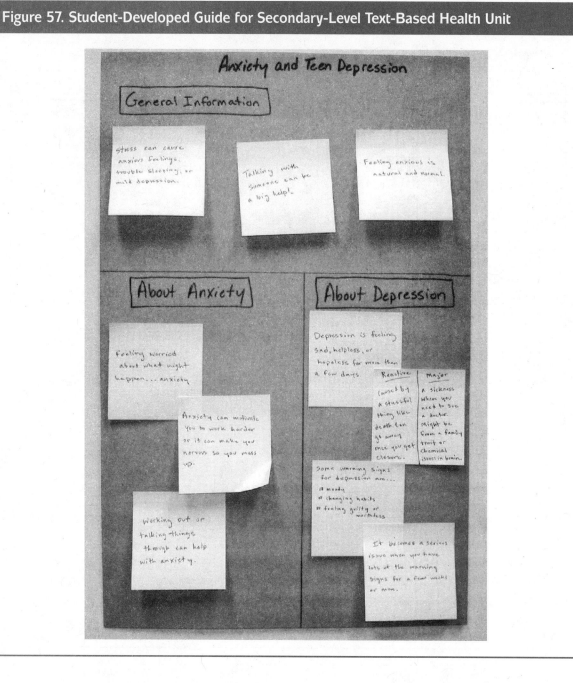

topically related headings, as shown in the sample in Figure 57. The resulting format resembles a graphic organizer and is also similar to the Foldable Guide, a type of Manipulative Guide discussed in chapter 14. The student was then able to assemble and rearrange the sticky notes, using them as a movable means to study and learn the content. This illustrates how learning the notion of a Student-Developed Guide can be adapted and modified according to the variations in individual learning styles.

Tips for Diverse Learners

- Thoroughly model and think aloud examples.
- Encourage the use of sticky notes and pictorial information.
- Encourage labeling of key concepts.

REFERENCES

Manz, S.L. (2002). A strategy for previewing textbooks: Teaching readers to become THIEVES. *The Reading Teacher, 55,* 434–435.

Robinson, F.P. (1946). *Effective study.* New York: Harper & Brothers.

Taylor, D.B., & Wood, K.D. (2005). Activating study skills in the middle school classroom. *Middle School Journal, 36*(5), 51–55.

Wood, K.D., & Beattie, J. (2004). Meeting the literacy needs of students with ADHD in the middle school classroom. *Middle School Journal, 35*(3), 50–55.

Reproducibles

Teacher Checklist for Evaluating a Text

Evaluating the Text	YES	NO
Fiction		
Nonfiction		
Cause/Effect		
Descriptive/Definitions		
Compare/Contrast		
Sequential		
Problem/Solution		
Are related concepts introduced within a few pages?		
Can portions of the selection be skipped?		
Do some portions or sources require more thorough reading?		
Are other sources of information needed?		

Teacher Checklist for Evaluating the Reader

Evaluating the Reader— Reader needs support to:	YES	NO
Identify basic, explicitly stated ideas and/or details		
Understand author intent		
Identify propositions		
Identify descriptive words and phrases to support visualization		
Connect personal experiences with author clues to make inferences		
Identify and use major elements to synthesize the text		
Use collected inferences and personal insights to evaluate the major premise		
Summarize by scaffolding major ideas		
Take a critical stance		

Collaborative Listening–Viewing Guide

Class:

Topic:

Student's name:

Group members:

<u>Preview/Review</u>

<u>Record (individually)</u>   <u>Elaborate (groups)</u>

<u>Synthesize (whole class)</u>

Reciprocal Teaching Discussion Guide

Text Examined

Synopsis of Article

Predict

Make a prediction about each passage after you read the title.	Confirm or disconfirm your prediction.	Provide evidence from the book to support your thoughts.
1.	1.	1.
2.	2.	2.
3.	3.	3.
4.	4.	4.
5.	5.	5.

Read

Question	Question	Question
Discuss Pose your questions to the group.	⇓	⇓
Clarify Write any clarifications made by the group members.		

Summarize

Write two or three ideas you think are important to remember about this passage. Share these points with your group.

1.
2.
3.

Then, as a group, decide which of the ideas are the most important to include in a group summary of the passage. Write the summary below in three or four sentences.

Guiding Readers Through Text: Strategy Guides for New Times (2nd ed.) by Karen D. Wood, Diane Lapp, James Flood, and D. Bruce Taylor. © 2008 by the International Reading Association. May be copied for classroom use.

Critical Profiler Guide

After-Reading, Critical Stance Questions	Student Response After Reading	Student Follow-Up Alternative View (Choose One)

Inquiry Guide

Primary Topic:	Major Subtopics or Themes			Summary or synthesis of each text	Importance of information
What We Know					
Source 1:					1 2 3 4 5 Not Very Helpful Helpful
Source 2:					1 2 3 4 5 Not Very Helpful Helpful
Source 3:					1 2 3 4 5 Not Very Helpful Helpful
Summary of each subtopic or theme					

Learning-From-Text Guide
for Intermediate-Level Lessons

Instructions: Read pages _____ in _____ and answer the following questions with a partner.

A. Literal Level (answers found in the book)
1.
2.
3.
4.
5.

B. Inferential Level (Think about what you read and search for the answer; it may be found as the main idea of a paragraph, or it may be why something was caused.)
1.
2.
3.
4.
5.

C. Generalization/Evaluative Level (Questions will be answered on your own by thinking and applying what you know about the topic.)
1.
2.
3.

Review: Think back to our class discussion on classifying questions. Below the following questions write the level (Literal, Inferential, or Generalization/Evaluative) each belongs to. After identifying each, turn to your partner and create at least one question for each level using the text you just read. These questions will be shared and charted with the class.

Part 1
1. Type of Question: _____

2. Type of Question: _____

3. Type of Question: _____

Part 2
Literal-Level Question: _____
_____

Inferential-Level Question: _____
_____

Generalization/Evaluative-Level Question: _____
_____

Guiding Readers Through Text: Strategy Guides for New Times (2nd ed.) by Karen D. Wood, Diane Lapp, James Flood, and D. Bruce Taylor. © 2008 by the International Reading Association. May be copied for classroom use.

Learning-From-Text Guide for Secondary-Level Lessons

Instructions: Read pages _____ in _____ and answer the following questions on your own. When you have completed all the answers on this strategy guide, meet with a partner and compare your answers. If there are any discrepancies between your answers, go back to the text and highlight the information that supports your answer. If you find new information that discredits your answer, make the necessary changes so that it is correct.

When comparisons are complete, fill in the accompanying chart by copying each question under the appropriate heading. For example, if the question is a Literal-Level question and the answer is easily found straight from the text, then copy the question in the heading "Literal Level."

1.

2.

3.

4.

5.

6.

7.

8.

9.

10.

Literal Level In the Book—Right There	Inferential Level In the Book— Think & Search	Generalization/ Evaluative Level In My Head—Author & Me In My Head—On My Own

Multiple-Source Research Guide

Instructions: Indicate the sources chosen and draw/chart/write what you have learned.

Name:

Group members:

Our research topic is:

I am/we are researching the following sources:

Source/Reference 1:

Subtopic 1:

Source/Reference 2:

Subtopic 2:

Source/Reference 3:

Subtopic 3:

Anticipation Guide for Preschool and Primary Grades

Title _____ Author _____

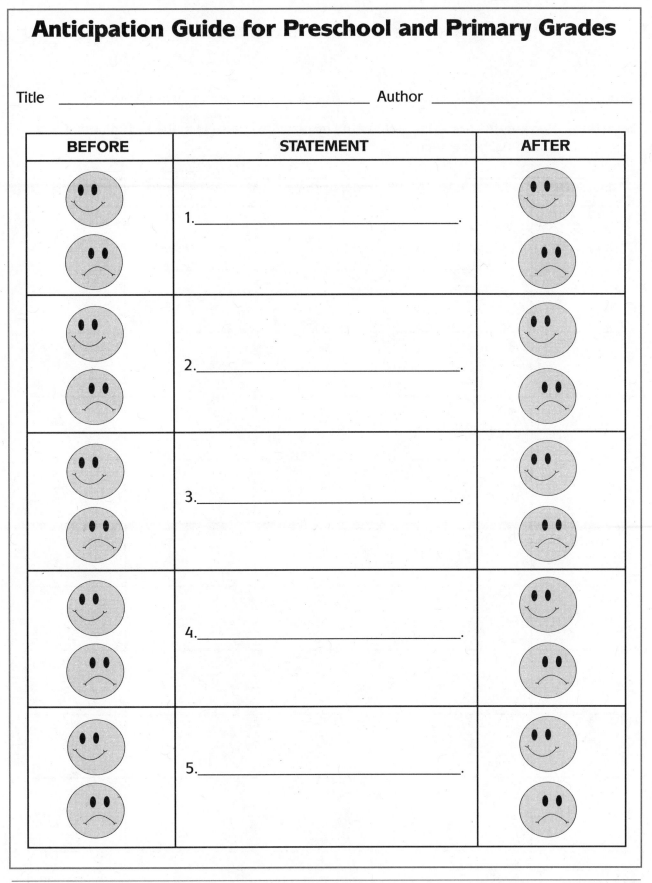

BEFORE	STATEMENT	AFTER
	1._____.	
	2._____.	
	3._____.	
	4._____.	
	5._____.	

Anticipation Guide for Elementary Level

Topic:

Directions: React to the following statements by placing a plus (+) in the left column if you agree or a minus (–) if you disagree.

BEFORE	STATEMENT	AFTER
	1.	
	2.	
	3.	
	4.	
	5.	
	6.	
	7.	
	8.	
	9.	
	10.	

Anticipation Guide for Intermediate and Secondary Levels

Topic/Title:

Directions: Take turns reading each of these statements with your partner. In the "Before" column, put a plus (+) if you agree with the statement or a minus (–) if you disagree. Make sure you justify your reactions with personal experiences, ideas, events, or analogies. After reading, return to the statements by marking what the story says and indicate in the "After" column if you have changed your mind or broadened your views.

BEFORE	STATEMENT	AFTER	
		Author	You
	1.		
	2.		
	3.		
	4.		

Extended Anticipation Guide

Part 1: Read each statement and decide if you agree or disagree with it. Circle the character from the left-hand set that matches your views.

Decide		Statement	Reevaluate		Support Your View
Agree	Disagree		Agree	Disagree	
		1.			
		2.			
		3.			
		4.			
		5.			

Part 2: Visit each of the sites listed below and gather information through what you see, hear, and read about _____.

1.
2.
3.
4.
5.
6.

Part 3: Consider the information you have collected from the websites. Reevaluate the statements and then support your final conclusions with evidence from the website resources.

Reaction Review Guide

Names of Group Members:

Topic:

Directions: With your partner, take turns reading and discussing each of the statements below. Put a check if you agree or disagree with each statement. Be sure to support your answer with at least one example. Use your book or any other sources for support.

1. _____
   _____.

   _____ I agree   _____ I disagree

   because:

2. _____
   _____.

   _____ I agree   _____ I disagree

   because:

3. _____
   _____.

   _____ I agree   _____ I disagree

   because:

4. _____
   _____.

   _____ I agree   _____ I disagree

   because:

5. _____
   _____.

   _____ I agree   _____ I disagree

   because:

Directions for Creating a Flip Chart

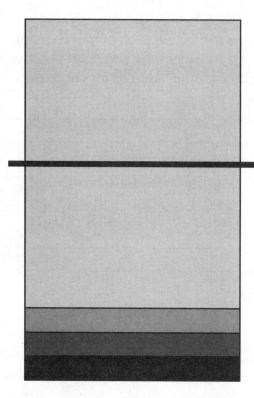 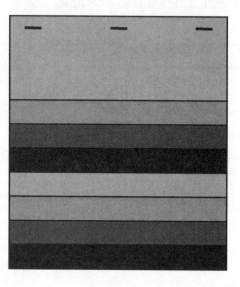

Step One: Stack 3 to 5 sheets of paper one on top of the other with a ½" overlap. The dotted line represents an imaginary fold line.

Step Two: Fold and crease from the top so that you create a flip chart with sheets evenly spaced at ½" intervals. Staple just below the fold.

Instructions for Folding and Assembling
an Origami Guide

Directions for Folding Paper

Directions for Gluing Paper Together

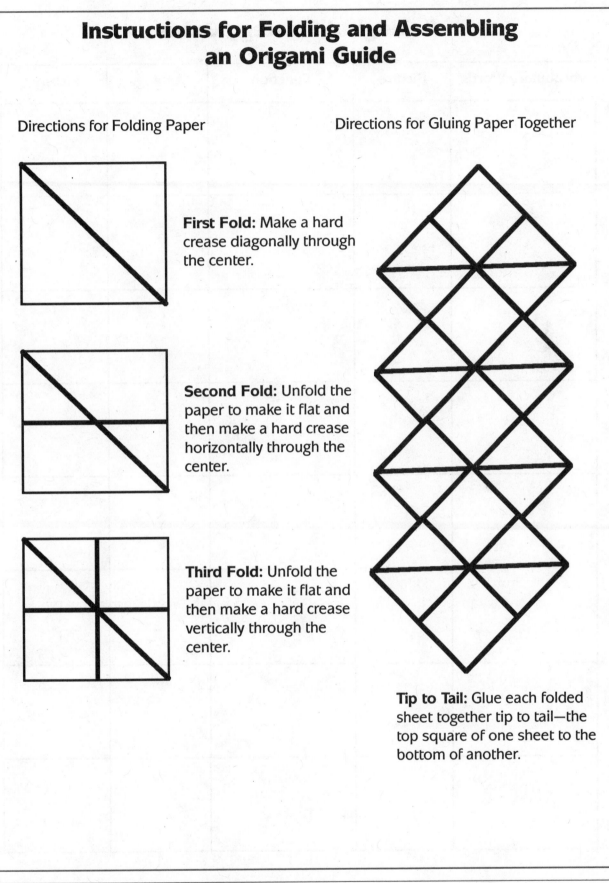

First Fold: Make a hard crease diagonally through the center.

Second Fold: Unfold the paper to make it flat and then make a hard crease horizontally through the center.

Third Fold: Unfold the paper to make it flat and then make a hard crease vertically through the center.

Tip to Tail: Glue each folded sheet together tip to tail—the top square of one sheet to the bottom of another.

Analogical Strategy Guide

Vocabulary Words	Picture	Function	Analogy	Picture

Analogical Strategy Guide for Student Creation

Follow the directions for each section.

1. Engage. In the following box, list all the words or ideas you think of when you hear _____. (You have three minutes to do this.)

2. Explore. With a partner, read each of the following vocabulary words. Go back to the text and find where the word is used; use context clues to decipher what each word means. In the box below write your working definition next to each word.

Vocabulary Word	Your Definition

3. Develop. Using the definitions you created for the vocabulary words above, create an Analogical Strategy Guide. To do this, reflect on the definitions you created, then in the following chart, create an analogy for each word to something of today's people and draw an appropriate picture if possible.

(continued)

Analogical Strategy Guide for Student Creation
(continued)

Vocabulary Words	Picture	Function	Analogy	Picture

4. **Apply.** Refer back to the Analogical Strategy Guide you made as well as the definitions for the vocabulary words you thought of with your partner. Applying the knowledge you have of these words, write a paragraph (narrative or expository) using at least four of the new vocabulary words correctly. The words should be used so that if a person who had no prior knowledge of the vocabulary were to read your paragraph he or she would be able to determine what the words meant by using the context clues you have given.

Guiding Readers Through Text: Strategy Guides for New Times (2nd ed.) by Karen D. Wood, Diane Lapp, James Flood, and D. Bruce Taylor. © 2008 by the International Reading Association. May be copied for classroom use.

True/False Concept Guide

Part 1. Directions: Place each of these statements under either the "true" or the "false" heading.

True

False

_____

_____

_____

_____

True

False

_____   _____

_____   _____

_____   _____

_____   _____

Part 2. Directions: From the information given in the text, complete a closed sort by placing each word or phrase from the word bank under the correct heading.

Headings

_____ _____ _____

Word Bank

_____ _____ _____

_____ _____ _____

Concept Guide

Topic:

Part 1. Directions: On your own, complete the following Cornell Notes–inspired strategy guide as you read. Remember what we have learned about Cornell Notes as you fill in the chart and also that we are working to recognize and categorize main ideas from the supporting details. You can always incorporate supporting details in the summary section of the guide, because it may not be necessary to include these in the main portion. When you are done with your reading and have completed the Cornell Notes, meet with your group and compare notes; if you are missing any important details or have any new questions, add them to your guide.

Cue Column:	Note-Taking Column:

Summary:

(continued)

Concept Guide (continued)

Part 2. Directions: Read the selected portion of the text from _____ on your own. Then, in groups, discuss each printed statement below and place a checkmark next to the ones that are specifically supported by the text you just read.

___1. _____

___2. _____

___3. _____

___4. _____

___5. _____

___6. _____

Part 3. Directions: Working with your group, use the information in Parts 1 and 2 to create a timeline that highlights _____. Your timeline should include _____ _____. When complete, you should have at least 10 of the most important dates or events included on your timeline.

_____

_____

_____

_____

_____

_____

_____

Pattern Guide Illustrating
Cause-and-Effect Relationships

Cause   **Effect**

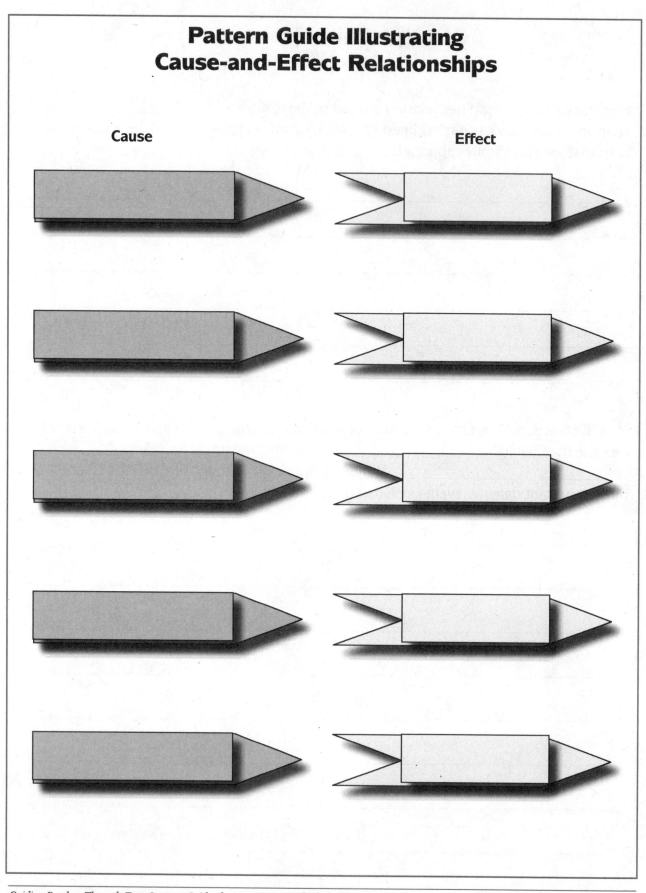

Pattern Guide

Topic:

I. Directions: Read the section in _____ on _____ (pages ___–
___). As you read, write three important points relating to each of the following topics.

A.

    1.

    2.

    3.

B.

    1.

    2.

    3.

C.

    1.

    2.

    3.

II. Directions: Using the information given in the text,

_____

_____

_____

_____.

(continued)

Guiding Readers Through Text: Strategy Guides for New Times (2nd ed.) by Karen D. Wood, Diane Lapp, James Flood, and D. Bruce Taylor.
© 2008 by the International Reading Association. May be copied for classroom use.

Pattern Guide (continued)

1		
2		
3		
4		
5		
6		

III. Directions: From the information you gathered above, we can begin to build connections among various concepts. In this section, we will be examining the causes (why something happens) and the effects (what happened) of concepts. Match each cause on the left with the appropriate effect on the right by writing the letter of the effect on the appropriate line.

Examples:

Cause   Effect

1. _____   1. _____

2. _____   2. _____

3. _____   3. _____

Exercise:

Cause   Effect

1. _____   1. _____

2. _____   2. _____

3. _____   3. _____

Process Guide Bookmark

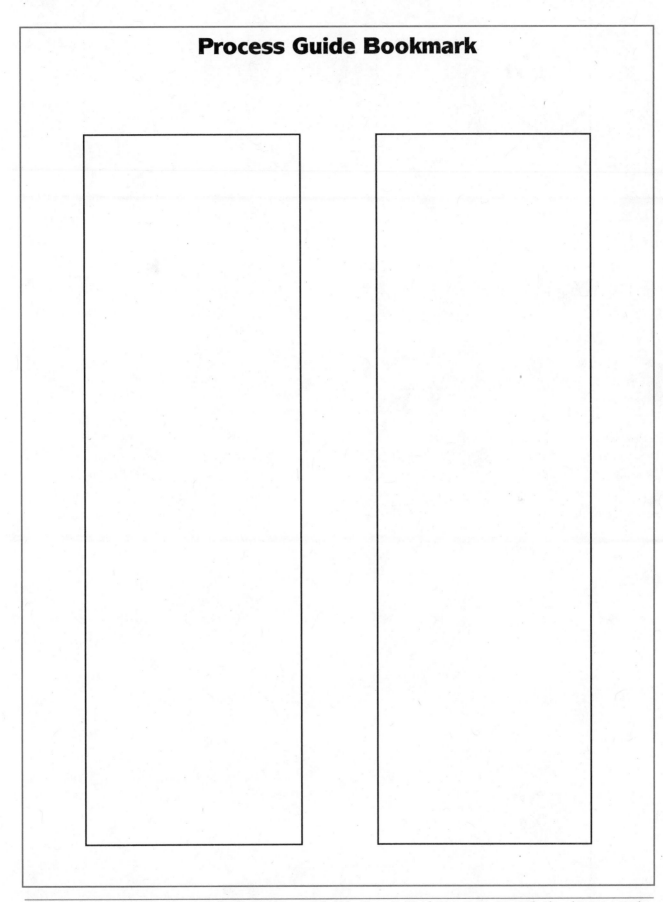

Note. Page numbers followed by *f*, *t*, or *r* indicate *figures*, *tables*, or *reproducibles* respectively.

REYES, C., 27
RICHGELS, D.J., 145
RICKARDS, J.P., 5
RIFE, A., 8
RILEY, J.D., 5
ROBINSON, F.P., 167
ROLLER, C.M., 10
ROSENBLATT, L.M., 53
ROSENSHINE, B.V., 22
ROTHKOPF, E.Z., 5
RUSS, P., 26

S

SAUL, E.W., 7
SCAFFOLDING, 10–11; for Student-Developed Guide, 168
SCIENCE: Analogical Strategy Guide for, 124, 125*f*; Anticipation Guide for, 92, 92*f*;
    Collaborative Listening Viewing Guide for, 34–36, 35*f*; Concept Guide for,
    131–132, 133*f*; Extended Anticipation Guide for, 96, 97*f*–98*f*; Inquiry Guide for,
    62, 63*f*–64*f*; Learning-From-Text Guide for, 68–70, 69*f*; Origami Guide for,
    119–120; Pattern Guide for, 139*f*, 141*f*–142*f*; Point-Of-View Guide for, 78, 84;
    Reading Road Map for, 156, 157*f*–158*f*; Textbook Activity Guide for, 162, 163*f*
SELF-MONITORING: in Textbook Activity Guide, 161
SILLS, T., 26
SINGER, H., 16, 65–66, 123–124, 126
SKIMMING, 26
SMID, K., 5
SMITH, M.C., 7
SMITH, SARA, 111–112
SMYLIE, M.A., 10
SOARES, LINA, 53, 57, 59
SOCIALLY CONSTRUCTED KNOWLEDGE: strategy guides and, 9–10
SOCIAL STUDIES: Analogical Strategy Guide for, 127*f*–129*f*; Critical Profiler Guide for,
    54–58, 57*f*, 59*f*; Extended Anticipation Guide for, 96, 98, 99*f*; Interactive
    Reading Guide for, 38–40, 39*f*–41*f*; Multiple-Source Research Guide for, 74, 76*f*;
    Point-Of-View Guide for, 79. *See also* history
SOCIAL STUDIES HELP CENTER, 56
SOTO, G., 92
SPENCER, B.H., 123, 126
SQ3R. *See* Survey, Question, Read, Recite, Review
STATEMENT GUIDES, 87–103
STRATEGIC READERS: development of, strategy guides and, 10–11; encouraging, 27
STRATEGY GUIDE(S): getting started with, 15–28; limitations of, 17; modeling use of,
    20–24; moving to, 8–12, 9*f*; selection of, 16–20; term, xiii; types and features of,
    21*t*–22*t*; using in classrooms, 1–28. *See also* study guide(s)
STUDENT-DEVELOPED GUIDE, 167–171, 169*f*–170*f*
STUDY GUIDE(S), 3–14; definition of, 4–5; evidence for, 5; moving to strategy guides,
    8–12, 9*f*; for new times, 5–7. *See also* strategy guide(s)
SUBSTANTIATION: in Extended Anticipation Guide, 96
SUMMARIZING: in Inquiry Guide, 61–62; in reciprocal teaching, 45–46
SURVEY, QUESTION, READ, RECITE, REVIEW (SQ3R), 168
SYNTHESIZING: in Collaborative Listening-Viewing Guide, 34

T

TABBED BOOKS, 110, 110*f*

TAG. *See* Textbook Activity Guide

TAYLOR, D.B., xiv, 11, 31, 73, 168

TEXT: evaluation of, 17–19, 18*f*, 174*r*; Pattern Guide on, 137; pattern signals in, 138*f*

TEXTBOOK(S): inconsiderate, 16; versus multiliteracies, xiii; Student-Developed Guide for, 167

TEXTBOOK ACTIVITY GUIDE (TAG), 161–163, 163*f*

TEXT STRUCTURE GUIDES, 121–142

THIEVES STRATEGY, 168

THINKING GUIDES, 51–85

THOMAS, M.M., 3

THOUGHTFUL LITERACY: term, xiv, 8

TIERNEY, R.J., 5

TINAJERO, J., 25

TOPIC: in Inquiry Guide, 61

TOTTEN, S., 26

TRIER, J., 6

TRI-FOLDS, 110–112, 112*f*

TURNER, J.C., 10

TUTTLE, M., 5

V

VACCA, J.A.L., 3, 5, 27, 89, 107, 137

VACCA, R.T., xi, 3, 5, 27, 89, 107, 137

VARELAS, M., 8

VAUGHN, S., 45

VIEWING: Collaborative Listening-Viewing Guide, 31–36, 35*f*, 176*r*

VOCABULARY: Analogical Strategy Guide for, 123–129; Glossing on, 146; Process Guide and, 152–153, 152*f*

VYGOTSKY, L.S., xiv, 9–10, 62

W

WALLER, T.G., 5

WASHBURNE, J.N., 5

WHITE, S., 145

WILLIAMS, L.E., 118

WIXSON, K.K., 10, 27

WOMACK, S., 5

WOOD, K.D., xiii, xiv, 4–6, 8–9, 11, 25, 31–33, 35, 37, 40–43, 73, 75, 77, 79, 81–82, 84, 95, 103, 155, 157–158, 163, 167–169

WRITING: with Extended Anticipation Guide, 98

Y

YOWELL, C.M., 10

Z

ZICK, TY, 108

ZIKE, D., 107

ZONE OF PROXIMAL DEVELOPMENT (ZPD), 9–10